HAVAMAL

OLD NORSE
3 ENGLISH TRANSLATIONS

HUGINN & MUNINN PUBLISHING

The Pocket Study Havamal™ Carrie Overton

1st Edition ©2017 Carrie Overton

ISBN: 978-1-937571-34-4

All rights reserved.
This book or any portion thereof may not be reproduced or used in any manner whatsoever without the express written permission of the publisher except for the use of brief quotations in a book review.

For information on
Asatru and Germanic Heathenry
please visit our website:

huginnandmuninn.net

Hail the Aesir!
Hail the Vanir!
Hail the Folk!

Publishers Note:

Various translators chose to lay out the poem differently from one another and the three translations stanzas in my book eventually diverge from one another.

Due to this I have placed the stanzas in the same order that relates to how the Old Norse was written but have left the numbering correct for your reference.

For example, you may see on one page stanza 136 followed by stanza 138 and then followed by stanza 135 and so on.

This is not an error.

This was done intentionally to keep continuity with the Old Norse.

You will find upon reading the stanzas that they are all the same stanza even though they are numbered differently.

Carrie

HAVAMAL

1. Gáttir allar,
áðr gangi fram,
um skoðask skyli,
um skyggnast skyli,
því at óvíst er at vita,
hvar óvinir
sitja á fleti fyrir.

1. At every door-way,
ere one enters,
one should spy round,
one should pry round
for uncertain is the witting
that there be no foeman sitting,
within, before one on the floor.
BRAY

1. All door-ways,
before going forward, should be looked to;
for difficult it is to know where foes may sit
within a dwelling.
THORPE

1. Within the gates ere a man shall go,
(Full warily let him watch,)
Full long let him look about him;
For little he knows where a foe may lurk,
And sit in the seats within.
BELLOWS

2. Gefendr heilir!
Gestr er inn kominn,
hvar skal sitja sjá?
Mjök er bráðr,
sá er á bröndum skal
síns of freista frama.

2. Hail, ye Givers! a guest is come;
say! where shall he sit within?
Much pressed is he who fain on the hearth
would seek for warmth and weal.
BRAY

2. Givers, hail!
A guest is come in:
where shall he sit?
In much hast is he,
who on the ways has
to try his luck.
THORPE

2. Hail to the giver! A guest has come;
Where shall the stranger sit?
Swift shall he be who with swords shall try
The proof of his might to make.
BELLOWS

3. Elds er þörf,
þeims inn er kominn
ok á kné kalinn;
matar ok váða
er manni þörf,
þeim er hefr um fjall farit.

3. He hath need of fire, who now is come,
numbed with cold to the knee;
food and clothing the wanderer craves
who has fared o'er the rimy fell.
BRAY

3. Fire is needful
to him who is come in,
and whose knees are frozen;
food and raiment
a man requires,
who o'er the fell has travelled.
THORPE

3. Fire he needs who with frozen knees,
has come from the cold without;
Food and clothes must the farer have,
The man from the mountains come.
BELLOWS

4. Vatns er þörf,
þeim er til verðar kemr,
þerru ok þjóðlaðar,
góðs of æðis,
ef sér geta mætti,
orðs ok endrþögu.

4. He craves for water,
who comes for refreshment,
drying and friendly bidding,
marks of good will, fair fame if 'tis won,
and welcome once and again.
BRAY

4. Water to him is needful
who for refection comes,
a towel and hospitable invitation,
a good reception;
if he can get it,
discourse and answer.
THORPE

4. Water and towels and welcoming speech,
should he find who comes to the feast;
If renown he would get, and again be greeted,
Wisely and well must he act.
BELLOWS

5. Vits er þörf,
þeim er víða ratar;
dælt er heima hvat;
at augabragði verðr,
sá er ckki kann
ok með snotrum sitr.

5. He hath need of his wits who wanders
wide, aught simple will serve at home;
but a gazing-stock is the fool who sits
mid the wise, and nothing knows.
BRAY

5. Wit is needful
to him who travels far:
at home all is easy.
A laughing-stock is he
who nothing knows,
and with the instructed sits.
THORPE

5. Wits must he have who wanders wide.
But all is easy at home;
At the witless man the wise shall wink,
when among such men he sits.
BELLOWS

6. At hyggjandi sinni
skyli-t maðr hræsinn vera,
heldr gætinn at geði;
þá er horskr ok þögull
kemr heimisgarða til,
sjaldan verðr víti vörum,
því at óbrigðra vin
fær maðr aldregi
en mannvit mikit.

6. Let no man glory in the greatness of his mind,
but rather keep watch o'er his wits.
Cautious and silent let him enter a dwelling;
to the heedful comes seldom harm,
for none can find a more faithful friend
than the wealth of mother wit.
BRAY

6. Of his understanding
no one should be proud,
but rather in conduct cautious.
When the prudent and taciturn
come to a dwelling,
harm seldom befalls the cautious;
for a firmer friend
no man ever gets
than great sagacity.
THORPE

6. A man shall not boast of his keenness of mind, but keep it close in his breast;
To the silent and wise does ill come seldom, when he goes as guest to a house;
(For a faster friend one never finds than wisdom tried and true.)
BELLOWS

7. Inn vari gestr,
er til verðar kemr,
þunnu hljóði þegir,
eyrum hlýðir,
en augum skoðar;
svá nýsisk fróðra hverr fyrir.

7. Let the wary stranger who seeks refreshment
keep silent with sharpened hearing;
with his ears let him listen, and look with his
eyes; thus each wise man spies out the way.
BRAY

7. A way guest
who to refection comes,
keeps a cautious silence,
(Or/Wit is needful
to him who travels far:
harm seldom befalls the wary;)
with his hears listens,
and with his eyes observes:
so explores every prudent man.
THORPE

7. The knowing guest who goes to the feast,
In silent attention sits;
With his ears he hears,
with his eyes he watches,
Thus wary are wise men all.
BELLOWS

8. Hinn er sæll,
er sér of getr
lof ok líknstafi;
ódælla er við þat,
er maðr eiga skal
annars brjóstum í.

8. Happy is he who wins for himself
fair fame and kindly words;
but uneasy is that which a man doth own
while it lies in another's breast.
BRAY

8. He is happy,
who for himself obtains
fame and kind words:
less sure is that
which a man must have
in another's breast.
THORPE

8. Happy the one who wins for himself,
favor and praises fair;
Less safe by far is the wisdom found,
that is hid in another's heart.
BELLOWS

9. Sá er sæll,
er sjalfr of á
lof ok vit, meðan lifir;
því at ill ráð
hefr maðr oft þegit
annars brjóstum ór.

9. Happy is he who hath in himself
praise and wisdom in life;
for oft doth a man ill counsel get
when 'tis born in another's breast.
BRAY

9. He is happy,
who in himself possesses
fame and wit while living;
for bad counsels
have oft been received
from another's breast.
THORPE

9. Happy the man,
who has while he lives,
wisdom and praise as well,
For evil counsel a man full oft has,
from another's heart.
BELLOWS

10. Byrði betri
berr-at maðr brautu at
en sé mannvit mikit;
auði betra
þykkir þat í ókunnum stað;
slíkt er válaðs vera.

10. A better burden can no man bear
on the way than his mother wit;
'tis the refuge of the poor,
and richer it seems than wealth in a world
untried.

10. A better burden
no man bears on the way
than much good sense;
that is thought better than riches
in a strange place;
such is the recourse of the indigent.
THORPE

10. A better burden may no man bear,
for wanderings wide than wisdom;
It is better than wealth on unknown ways,
And in grief a refuge it gives.
BELLOWS

11. Byrði betri
berr-at maðr brautu at
en sé mannvit mikit;
vegnest verra
vegr-a hann velli at
en sé ofdrykkja öls.

11. A better burden can no man bear
on the way than his mother wit:
and no worse provision can he carry with him
than too deep a draught of ale.
BRAY

11. A worse provision
on the way he cannot carry
than too much beer-bibbing;
so good is not,
as it is said,
beer for the sons of men.
THORPE

11. A better burden may no man bear,
for wanderings wide than wisdom;
Worse food for the journey he brings,
not afield than an over-drinking of ale.
BELLOWS

12. Er-a svá gótt
sem gótt kveða
öl alda sona,
því at færa veit,
er fleira drekkr
síns til geðs gumi.

12. Less good than they say for the sons of
men is the drinking oft of ale:
for the more they drink, the less can they
think and keep a watch o'er their wits.
BRAY

12. A worse provision
no man can take from table
than too much beer-bibbing:
for the more he drinks
the less control he has
of his own mind.
THORPE

12. Less good there lies,
than most believe in ale for mortal men;
For the more he drinks the less does man
Of his mind the mastery hold.
BELLOWS

13. Óminnishegri heitir
sá er yfir öldrum þrumir,
hann stelr geði guma;
þess fugls fjöðrum
ek fjötraðr vark
í garði Gunnlaðar.

13. A bird of Unmindfulness flutters o'er ale
feasts, wiling away men's wits:
with the feathers of that fowl I was fettered
once in the garths of Gunnlods below.
BRAY

13. Oblivion's heron 'tis called
that over potations hovers,
he steals the minds of men.
With this bird's pinions I was fettered
in Gunnlöds dwelling.
THORPE

13. Over beer the bird of forgetfulness broods,
and steals the minds of men;
With the heron's feathers fettered I lay
And in Gunnloth's house was held.
BELLOWS

14. Ölr ek varð,
varð ofrölvi
at ins fróða Fjalars;
því er ölðr bazt,
at aftr of heimtir
hverr sitt geð gumi.

14. Drunk was I then, I was over drunk
in that crafty Jötun's court.
But best is an ale feast when man is able
to call back his wits at once.
BRAY

14. Drunk I was,
I was over-drunk,
at that cunning Fjalar's.
It's the best drunkenness,
when every one after it
regains his reason.
THORPE

14. Drunk I was,
I was dead-drunk,
when with Fjalar wise I was;
'Tis the best of drinking,
if back one brings his wisdom,
with him home.
BELLOWS

15. Þagalt ok hugalt
skyli þjóðans barn
ok vígdjarft vera;
glaðr ok reifr
skyli gumna hverr,
unz sinn bíðr bana.

15. Silent and thoughtful and bold in strife
the prince's bairn should be.
Joyous and generous let each man show him
until he shall suffer death.
BRAY

15. Taciturn and prudent,
and in war daring
should a king's children be;
joyous and liberal
every one should be
until the hour of his death.
THORPE

15. The son of a king,
shall be silent and wise,
and bold in battle as well;
Bravely and gladly a man shall go,
till the day of his death is come.
BELLOWS

16. Ósnjallr maðr
hyggsk munu ey lifa,
ef hann við víg varask;
en elli gefr
hánum engi frið,
þótt hánum geirar gefi.

16. A coward believes he will ever live
if he keep him safe from strife:
but old age leaves him not long in peace
though spears may spare his life.
BRAY

16. A cowardly man
thinks he will ever live,
if warfare he avoids;
but old age will
give him no peace,
though spears may spare him.
THORPE

16. The sluggard,
believes he shall live forever.
If the fight he faces not;
But age shall not grant him the gift of peace,
though spears may spare his life.
BELLOWS

17. Kópir afglapi
er til kynnis kemr,
þylsk hann um eða þrumir;
allt er senn,
ef hann sylg of getr,
uppi er þá geð guma.

17. A fool will gape when he goes to a friend,
and mumble only, or mope;
but pass him the ale cup and all in a moment
the mind of that man is shown.
BRAY

17. A fool gapes
when to a house he comes,
to himself mutters or is silent;
but all at once,
if he gets drink,
then is the man's mind displayed.
THORPE

17. The fool is agape,
when he comes to the feast,
he stammers or else is still;
But soon if he gets a drink,
is it seen what the mind of the man is like.
BELLOWS

18. Sá einn veit
er víða ratar
ok hefr fjölð of farit,
hverju geði
stýrir gumna hverr,
sá er vitandi er vits.

18. He knows alone who has wandered wide,
and far has fared on the way,
what manner of mind a man doth own
who is wise of head and heart.
BRAY

18. He alone knows
who wanders wide,
and has much experienced,
by what disposition
each man is ruled,
who common sense possesses.
THORPE

18. He alone is aware who has wandered wide,
and far abroad has fared,
how great a mind is guided by him,
that wealth of wisdom has.
BELLOWS

19. Haldi-t maðr á keri,
drekki þó at hófi mjöð,
mæli þarft eða þegi,
ókynnis þess
vár þik engi maðr,
at þú gangir snemma at sofa.

19. Keep not the mead cup but drink thy
measure; speak needful words or none:
none shall upbraid thee for lack of breeding
if soon thou seek'st thy rest.
BRAY

19. Let a man hold the cup,
yet of the mead drink moderately,
speak sensibly or be silent.
As of a fault no man will admonish thee,
if thou goest betimes to sleep.
THORPE

19. Shun not the mead,
but drink in measure;
Speak to the point or be still;
For rudeness none shall rightly blame thee,
if soon thy bed thou seekest.
BELLOWS

20. Gráðugr halr,
nema geðs viti,
etr sér aldrtrega;
oft fær hlægis,
er með horskum kemr,
manni heimskum magi.

20. A greedy man, if he be not mindful,
eats to his own life's hurt:
oft the belly of the fool,
will bring him to scorn
when he seeks the circle of the wise.
BRAY

20. A greedy man,
if he be not moderate,
eats to his mortal sorrow.
Oftentimes his belly
draws laughter on a silly man,
who among the prudent comes.
THORPE

20. The greedy man,
if his mind be vague,
will eat till sick he is;
The vulgar man,
when among the wise,
to scorn by his belly is brought.
BELLOWS

21. Hjarðir þat vitu,
nær þær heim skulu,
ok ganga þá af grasi;
en ósviðr maðr
kann ævagi
síns of mál maga.

21. Herds know the hour of their going home
and turn them again from the grass;
but never is found a foolish man
who knows the measure of his maw.
BRAY

21. Cattle know
when to go home,
and then from grazing cease;
but a foolish man
never knows
his stomach's measure.
THORPE

21. The herds know,
well when home they shall fare,
and then from the grass they go;
But the foolish man,
his belly's measure,
shall never know aright.
BELLOWS

22. Vesall maðr
ok illa skapi
hlær at hvívetna;
hittki hann veit,
er hann vita þyrfti,
at hann er-a vamma vanr.

22. The miserable man and evil minded
makes of all things mockery,
and knows not that which he best should
know, that he is not free from faults.
BRAY

22. A miserable man,
and ill-conditioned,
sneers at every thing;
one thing he knows not,
which he ought to know,
that he is not free from faults.
THORPE

22. A paltry man,
and poor of mind,
at all things ever mocks;
For never he knows,
what he ought to know,
that he is not free from faults.
BELLOWS

23. Ósviðr maðr
vakir um allar nætr
ok hyggr at hvívetna;
þá er móðr,
er at morgni kemr,
allt er víl sem var.

23. The unwise man is awake all night,
and ponders everything over;
when morning comes he is weary in mind,
and all is a burden as ever.
BRAY

23. A foolish man
is all night awake,
pondering over everything;
he than grows tired;
and when morning comes,
all is lament as before.
THORPE

23. The witless man,
is awake all night,
thinking of many things;
Care-worn he is when the morning comes,
and his woe is just as it was.
BELLOWS

39. Fannk-a ek mildan mann
eða svá matar góðan,
að væri þiggja þegið,
eða síns fjár
svági [glöggvan],
að leið sé laun, ef þægi.

39. I found none so noble
or free with his food,
who was not gladdened with a gift,
nor one who gave of his gifts such store
but he loved reward, could he win it.
BRAY

39. I have never found a man so bountiful,
or so hospitable that he refused a present;
of his property so liberal
that he scorned a recompense.
THORPE

40. None so free with gifts or food,
have I found that gladly he took not a gift.
Nor one who so widely scattered his wealth
That of recompense hatred he had.
BELLOWS

40. Fjár síns,
er fengið hefr,
skyli-t maðr þörf þola;
oft sparir leiðum,
það er hefr ljúfum hugat;
margt gengr verr en varir.

40. Let no man stint him
and suffer need of the wealth
he has won in life;
oft is saved for a foe
what was meant for a friend,
and much goes worse than one weens.
BRAY

40. Of the property
which he has gained
no man should suffer need;
for the hated oft is spared
what for the dear was destined.
Much goes worse than is expected.
THORPE

39. If wealth a man has won for himself,
let him never suffer in need;
Oft he saves for a foe,
what he plans for a friend,
for much goes worse than we wish.
BELLOWS

41. Vápnum ok váðum
skulu vinir gleðjask;
þat er á sjalfum sýnst;
viðrgefendr ok endrgefendr
erusk lengst vinir,
ef þat bíðr at verða vel.

41. With raiment and arms
shall friends gladden each other,
so has one proved oneself;
for friends last longest, if fate be fair
who give and give again.
BRAY

41. With arms and vestments
friends should each other gladden,
those which are in themselves most sightly.
Givers and requiters are longest friends,
if all (else) goes well.
THORPE

41. Friends shall gladden each other,
with arms and garments,
as each for himself can see;
Gift-givers' friendships are longest found,
if fair their fates may be.
BELLOWS

42. Vin sínum
skal maðr vinr vera
ok gjalda gjöf við gjöf;
hlátr við hlátri
skyli höldar taka
en lausung við lygi.

42. To his friend a man
should bear him as friend,
and gift for gift bestow,
laughter for laughter let him exchange,
but leasing pay for a lie.
BRAY

42. To his friend
a man should be a friend,
and gifts with gifts requite.
Laughter with laughter
men should receive,
but leasing with lying.
THORPE

42. To his friend,
a man a friend shall prove,
and gifts with gifts requite;
But men shall mocking
with mockery answer,
and fraud with falsehood meet.
BELLOWS

43. Vin sínum
skal maðr vinr vera,
þeim ok þess vin;
en óvinar síns
skyli engi maðr
vinar vinr vera.

43. To his friend a man
should bear him as friend,
to him and a friend of his;
but let him beware
that he be not the friend
of one who is friend to his foe.
BRAY

43. To his friend
a man should be a friend,
to him and to his friend;
but of his foe
no man shall
the friend's friend be.
THORPE

43. To his friend,
a man a friend shall prove,
to him and the friend of his friend;
But never a man,
shall friendship make,
with one of his foeman's friends.
BELLOWS

44. Veiztu, ef þú vin átt,
þann er þú vel trúir,
ok vill þú af hánum gótt geta,
geði skaltu við þann blanda
ok gjöfum skipta,
fara at finna oft.

44. Hast thou a friend whom thou trustest
well, from whom thou cravest good?
Share thy mind with him,
gifts exchange with him,
fare to find him oft.
BRAY

44. Know, if thou has a friend
whom thou fully trustest,
and from whom thou woulds't good derive,
thou shouldst blend thy mind with his,
and gifts exchange,
and often go to see him.
THORPE

44. If a friend thou hast,
whom thou fully wilt trust,
and good from him wouldst get,
thy thoughts with his mingle,
and gifts shalt
thou make,
and fare to find him oft.
BELLOWS

45. Ef þú átt annan,
þanns þú illa trúir,
vildu af hánum þó gótt geta,
fagrt skaltu við þann mæla
en flátt hyggja
ok gjalda lausung við lygi.

45. But hast thou one whom thou trustest ill
yet from whom thou cravest good?
Thou shalt speak him fair, but falsely think,
and leasing pay for a lie.
BRAY

45. If thou hast another,
whom thou little trustest,
yet wouldst good from him derive,
thou shouldst speak him fair,
but think craftily,
and leasing pay with lying.
THORPE

45. If another thou hast whom thou hardly
wilt trust,
yet good from him wouldst get,
thou shalt speak him fair,
but falsely think,
and fraud with falsehood requite.
BELLOWS

46. Það er enn of þann
er þú illa trúir
ok þér er grunr at hans geði,
hlæja skaltu við þeim
ok um hug mæla;
glík skulu gjöld gjöfum.

46. Yet further of him whom thou trusted ill,
and whose mind thou dost misdoubt;
thou shalt laugh with him but withhold thy
thought, for gift with like gift should be paid.
BRAY

46. But of him yet further,
whom thou little trustest,
and thou suspectest his affection;
before him thou shouldst laugh,
and contrary to thy thoughts speak:
requital should the gift resemble.
THORPE

46. So is it with him whom thou hardly wilt
trust, and whose mind thou may not know;
Laugh with him mayst thou,
but speak not thy mind,
like gifts to his shalt thou give.
BELLOWS

47. Ungr var ek forðum,
fór ek einn saman,
þá varð ek villr vega;
auðigr þóttumk,
er ek annan fann,
maðr er manns gaman.

47. Young was I once, I walked alone,
and bewildered seemed in the way;
then I found me another and rich I thought me,
for man is the joy of man.
BRAY

47. I was once young,
I was journeying alone,
and lost my way;
rich I thought myself,
when I met another.
Man is the joy of man.
THORPE

47. Young was I once,
and wandered alone,
and naught of the road I knew;
Rich did I feel when a comrade I found,
for man is man's delight.
BELLOWS

48. Mildir, fræknir
menn bazt lifa,
sjaldan sút ala;
en ósnjallr maðr
uggir hotvetna,
sýtir æ glöggr við gjöfum.

48. Most blest is he who lives free and bold
and nurses never a grief,
for the fearful man is dismayed by aught,
and the mean one mourns over giving.
BRAY

48. Generous and brave men live best,
they seldom cherish sorrow;
but a base-minded man
dreads everything;
the niggardly is uneasy even at gifts.
THORPE

48. The lives of the brave and noble are best,
sorrows they seldom feed;
But the coward fear of all things feels,
and not gladly the niggard gives.
BELLOWS

49. Váðir mínar
gaf ek velli at
tveim trémönnum;
rekkar þat þóttusk,
er þeir rift höfðu;
neiss er nøkkviðr halr.

49. My garments once I gave in the field
to two land-marks made as men;
heroes they seemed when once they were clothed;
'tis the naked who suffer shame!
BRAY

49. My garments in a field
I gave away
to two wooden men:
heroes they seemed to be,
when they got cloaks:
exposed to insult is a naked man.
THORPE

49. My garments once,
in a field I gave to a pair of carven poles;
Heroes they seemed when clothes they had,
but the naked man is naught.
BELLOWS

50. Hrörnar þöll,
sú er stendr þorpi á,
hlýr-at henni börkr né barr;
svá er maðr,
sá er manngi ann.
Hvat skal hann lengi lifa?

50. The pine tree wastes which is perched on the hill,
nor bark nor needles shelter it;
such is the man whom none doth love;
for what should he longer live?
BRAY

50. A tree withers
that on a hill-top stands;
protects it neither bark nor leaves:
such is the man
whom no one favours:
why should he live long?
THORPE

50. On the hillside drear the fir-tree dies,
all bootless its needles and bark;
It is like a man whom no one loves.
Why should his life be long?
BELLOWS

51. Eldi heitari
brennr með illum vinum
friðr fimm daga,
en þá sloknar,
er inn sétti kemr,
ok versnar allr vinskapr.

51. Fiercer than fire among ill friends
for five days love will burn;
but anon 'tis quenched, when the sixth day comes,
and all friendship soon is spoiled.
BRAY

51. Hotter than fire
love for five days burns
between false friends;
but is quenched
when the sixth day comes,
and friendship is all impaired.
THORPE

51. Hotter than fire,
between false friends
does friendship five days burn;
When the sixth day comes the fire cools,
and ended is all the love.
BELLOWS

52. Mikit eitt
skal-a manni gefa;
oft kaupir sér í litlu lof,
með halfum hleif
ok með höllu keri
fekk ek mér félaga.

52. Not great things alone
must one give to another,
praise oft is earned for naught;
with half a loaf and a tilted bowl
I have found me many a friend.
BRAY

52. Something great
is not (always) to be given,
praise is often for a trifle bought.
With half a loaf
and a tilted vessel
I got myself a comrade
THORPE

52. No great thing needs a man to give,
oft little will purchase praise;
With half a loaf and a half-filled cup,
a friend full fast I made.
BELLOWS

53. Lítilla sanda
lítilla sæva
lítil eru geð guma;
því allir menn
urðu-t jafnspakir;
half er öld hvar.

53. Little the sand if little the seas,
little are minds of men,
for ne'er in the world were all equally wise,
'tis shared by the fools and the sage.
BRAY

53. Little are the sandgrains,
little the wits,
little the minds of (some) men;
for all men
are not wise alike:
men are everywhere by halves.
THORPE

53. A little sand has a little sea,
and small are the minds of men;
Though all men are not equal in wisdom,
yet half-wise only are all.
BELLOWS

54. Meðalsnotr
skyli manna hverr;
æva til snotr sé;
þeim er fyrða
fegrst at lifa,
er vel margt vitu.

54. Wise in measure let each man be;
but let him not wax too wise;
for never the happiest of men is he
who knows much of many things.
BRAY

54. Moderately wise
should each one be,
but never over-wise:
of those men
the lives are fairest,
who know much well.
THORPE

54. A measure of wisdom
each man shall have,
but never too much let him know;
The fairest lives do those men live,
whose wisdom wide has grown.
BELLOWS

55. Meðalsnotr
skyli manna hverr,
æva til snotr sé;
því at snotrs manns hjarta
verðr sjaldan glatt,
ef sá er alsnotr, er á.

55. Wise in measure should each man be;
but let him not wax too wise;
seldom a heart will sing with joy
if the owner be all too wise.
BRAY

55. Moderately wise
should each one be,
but never over-wise;
for a wise man's heart
is seldom glad,
if he is all-wise who owns it.
THORPE

55. A measure of wisdom each man shall have,
but never too much let him know;
For the wise man's heart is seldom happy,
if wisdom too great he has won.
BELLOWS

56. Meðalsnotr
skyli manna hverr,
æva til snotr sé;
örlög sín
viti engi fyrir,
þeim er sorgalausastr sefi.

56. Wise in measure should each man be,
but ne'er let him wax too wise:
who looks not forward to learn his fate
unburdened heart will bear.
BRAY

56. Moderately wise
should each one be,
but never over-wise.
His destiny let know
no man beforehand;
his mind will be freest from care.
THORPE

56. A measure of wisdom
each man shall have,
but never too much let him know;
Let no man the fate before him see,
for so is he freest from sorrow.
BELLOWS

57. Brandr af brandi
brenn, unz brunninn er,
funi kveikisk af funa;
maðr af manni
verðr at máli kuðr,
en til dælskr af dul.

57. Brand kindles from brand
until it be burned,
spark is kindled from spark,
man unfolds him by speech with man,
but grows over secret through silence.
BRAY

57. Brand burns from brand
until it is burnt out;
fire is from fire quickened.
Man to man
becomes known by speech,
but a fool by his bashful silence.
THORPE

57. A brand from a brand
is kindled and burned,
and fire from fire begotten;
And man by his speech is known to men,
and the stupid by their stillness.
BELLOWS

58. Ár skal rísa,
sá er annars vill
fé eða fjör hafa;
sjaldan liggjandi ulfr
lær of getr
né sofandi maðr sigr.

58. He must rise betimes who fain of another
or life or wealth would win;
scarce falls the prey to sleeping wolves,
or to slumberers victory in strife.
BRAY

58. He should early rise,
who another's property or life
desires to have.
Seldom a sluggish wolf
gets prey,
or a sleeping man victory.
THORPE

58. He must early go forth,
who fain the blood,
or the goods of another would get;
The wolf that lies idle shall win little meat,
or the sleeping man success.
BELLOWS

59. Ár skal rísa,
sá er á yrkjendr fáa,
ok ganga síns verka á vit;
margt of dvelr,
þann er um morgin sefr,
hálfr er auðr und hvötum.

59. He must rise betimes,
who hath few to serve him,
and see to his work himself;
who sleeps at morning is hindered much,
to the keen is wealth half-won.
BRAY

59. Early should rise
he who has few workers,
and go his work to see to;
greatly is he retarded
who sleeps the morn away,
wealth half depends on energy.
THORPE

59. He must early go forth,
whose workers are few,
himself his work to seek;
Much remains undone
for the morning-sleeper,
for the swift is wealth half won.
BELLOWS

60. Þurra skíða
ok þakinna næfra,
þess kann maðr mjöt,
þess viðar,
er vinnask megi
mál ok misseri.

60. Of dry logs saved and roof-bark stored
a man can know the measure,
of fire-wood too which should last him out
quarter and half years to come.
BRAY

60. Of dry planks
and roof-shingles
a man knows the measure;
of the fire-wood
that may suffice,
both measure and time.
THORPE

60. Of seasoned shingles and strips of bark,
for the thatch let one know his need,
and how much of wood he must have for a
month, or in half a year he will use.
BELLOWS

61. Þveginn ok mettr
ríði maðr þingi at,
þótt hann sé-t væddr til vel;
skúa ok bróka
skammisk engi maðr
né hests in heldr,
þótt hann hafi-t góðan

61. Fed and washed should one ride to court
though in garments none too new;
thou shalt not shame thee
for shoes or breeches,
nor yet for a sorry steed.
BRAY

61. Washed and fed,
let a man ride to the Thing,
although his garments be not too good;
of his shoes and breeches
let no one be ashamed,
nor of his horse,
although he have not a good one.
THORPE

61. Washed and fed to the council fare,
but care not too much for thy clothes;
Let none be ashamed of his shoes and hose,
less still of the steed he rides,
(Though poor be the horse he has.)
BELLOWS

62. Snapir ok gnapir,
er til sævar kemr,
örn á aldinn mar;
svá er maðr,
er með mörgum kemr
ok á formælendr fáa.

62. Like an eagle swooping over old ocean,
snatching after his prey,
so comes a man into court who finds
there are few to defend his cause.
BRAY

63. Gasps and gapes,
when to the sea he comes,
the eagles over old ocean;
so is a man,
who among many comes,
and has few advocates.
THORPE

62. When the eagle comes to the ancient sea,
he snaps and hangs his head;
So is a man in the midst of a throng,
who few to speak for him finds.
BELLOWS

63. Fregna ok segja
skal fróðra hverr,
sá er vill heitinn horskr;
einn vita
né annarr skal,
þjóð veit, ef þrír ro.

63. Each man who is wise and would wise be
called must ask and answer aright.
Let one know thy secret, but never a second,
if three a thousand shall know.
BRAY

62. Inquire and impart
should every man of sense,
who will be accounted sage.
Let one only know,
a second may not;
if three, all the world knows.
THORPE

63. To question and answer must all be ready,
who wish to be known as wise;
Tell one thy thoughts,
but beware of two,
all know what is known to three.
BELLOWS

64. Ríki sitt
skyli ráðsnotra
hverr í hófi hafa;
þá hann þat finnr,
er með fræknum kemr
at engi er einna hvatastr.

64. A wise counselled man,
will be mild in bearing
and use his might in measure,
lest when he comes among his fierce foes,
he finds others fiercer than he.
BRAY

64. His power should
every sagacious man
use with discretion;
for he will find,
when among the bold he comes,
that no one alone is the doughtiest.
THORPE

64. The man who is prudent,
a measured use of the might he has will make;
He finds when among the brave he fares,
that the boldest he may not be.
BELLOWS

65. orða þeira,
er maðr öðrum segir
oft hann gjöld of getr.

65. Each man should be watchful and wary in
speech, and slow to put faith in a friend,
for the words which one to another speaks
he may win reward of ill.
BRAY

65. Circumspect and reserved
every man should be,
and wary in trusting friends.
Of the words that a man says to another,
he often pays the penalty.
THORPE

65. Oft for the words,
that to others one speaks,
he will get but an evil gift.
BELLOWS

66. Mikilsti snemma
kom ek í marga staði,
en til síð í suma;
öl var drukkit,
sumt var ólagat,
sjaldan hittir leiðr í líð.

66. At many a feast I was far too late,
and much too soon at some;
drunk was the ale or yet unserved:
never hits he the joint who is hated.
BRAY

66. Much too early
I came to many places,
but too late to others;
the beer was drunk,
or not ready:
the disliked seldom hits the moment.
THORPE

66. Too early to many a meeting I came,
and some too late have I sought;
The beer was all drunk, or not yet brewed;
Little the loathed man finds.
BELLOWS

67. Hér ok hvar
myndi mér heim of boðit,
ef þyrftak at málungi mat,
eða tvau lær hengi
at ins tryggva vinar,
þars ek hafða eitt etit.

67. Here and there to a home I had haply
been asked had I needed no meat at my meals,
or were two hams left hanging in the house of
that friend where I had partaken of one.
BRAY

67. Here and there I should
have been invited,
if I a meal had needed;
or two hams had hung,
at that true friend's,
where of one I had eaten.
THORPE

67. To their homes men,
would bid me hither and yon,
if at meal-time I needed no meat,
or would hang two hams,
in my true friend's house,
where only one I had eaten.
BELLOWS

68. Eldr er beztr
með ýta sonum
ok sólar sýn,
heilyndi sitt,
ef maðr hafa nái̇r,
án við löst at lifa.

68. Most dear is fire to the sons of men,
most sweet the sight of the sun;
good is health if one can but keep it,
and to live a life without shame.
BRAY

68. Fire is best,
among the sons of men,
and the sight of the sun,
if his health a man can have,
with a life free from vice.
THORPE

68. Fire for men is the fairest gift,
and power to see the sun;
Health as well,
if a man may have it,
and a life not stained with sin.
BELLOWS

69. Er-at maðr alls vesall,
þótt hann sé illa heill;
sumr er af sonum sæll,
sumr af frændum,
sumr af fé ærnu,
sumr af verkum vel.

69. Not reft of all is he who is ill,
for some are blessed in their children,
some in their kin and some in their wealth,
and some in working well.
BRAY

69. No man lacks everything,
although his health be bad:
one in his sons is happy,
one in abundant wealth,
one in his good works.
THORPE

69. All wretched is no man,
though never so sick;
Some from their sons have joy,
some win it from kinsmen,
and some from their wealth,
and some from worthy works.
BELLOWS

70. Betra er lifðum
en sé ólifðum,
ey getr kvikr kú;
eld sá ek upp brenna
auðgum manni fyrir,
en úti var dauðr fyr durum.

70. More blest are the living than the lifeless,
'tis the living who come by the cow;
I saw the hearth-fire burn in the rich man's
hall and himself lying dead at the door.
BRAY

70. It is better to live,
even to live miserably;
a living man can always get a cow.
I saw fire consume
the rich man's property,
and death stood without his door.
THORPE

70. It is better to live than to lie a corpse,
the live man catches the cow;
I saw flames rise for the rich man's pyre,
and before his door he lay dead.
BELLOWS

71. Haltr ríðr hrossi,
hjörð rekr handar vanr,
daufr vegr ok dugir,
blindr er betri
en brenndr séi,
nýtr manngi nás.

71. The lame can ride horse, the handless
drive cattle, the deaf one can fight and prevail,
'tis happier for the blind than for him on the
bale-fire, but no man hath care for a corpse.
BRAY

71. The lame can ride on horseback,
the one-handed drive cattle;
the deaf fight and be useful:
to be blind is better
than to be burnt:
no ones gets good from a corpse.
THORPE

71. The lame rides a horse,
the handless is herdsman,
the deaf in battle is bold;
The blind man is better
than one that is burned,
no good can come of a corpse.
BELLOWS

72. Sonr er betri,
þótt sé síð of alinn
eftir genginn guma;
sjaldan bautarsteinar
standa brautu nær,
nema reisi niðr at nið.

72. Best have a son though he be late born
and before him the father be dead:
seldom are stones on the wayside raised
save by kinsmen to kinsmen.
BRAY

72. A son is better,
even if born late,
after his father's departure.
Gravestones seldom
stand by the way-side
unless raised by a kinsman to a kinsman.
THORPE

72. A son is better,
though late he be born,
and his father to death have fared;
Memory-stones seldom stand by the road,
save when kinsman honors his kin.
BELLOWS

73. Tveir ro eins herjar,
tunga er höfuðs bani;
er mér í heðin hvern
handar væni.

73. Two are hosts against one,
the tongue is the head's bane,
'neath a rough hide a hand may be hid;
BRAY

73. Two are adversaries:
the tongue is the bane of the head:
under every cloak
I expect a hand.
THORPE

73. Two make a battle,
the tongue slays the head;
In each furry coat a fist I look for.
BELLOWS

74. Nótt verðr feginn
sá er nesti trúir,
skammar ro skips ráar;
hverf er haustgríma;
fjölð of viðrir
á fimm dögum
en meira á mánuði.

*73 (Con.) He is glad at nightfall who knows
of his lodging, short is the ship's berth,
and changeful the autumn night,
much veers the wind ere the fifth day
and blows round yet more in a month.
BRAY

74. At night is joyful
he who is sure of travelling enjoyment.
(A ship's yards are short.)
Variable is an autumn night.
Many are the weather's changes
in five days, but more in a month.
THORPE

74. He welcomes the night
whose fare is enough,
(Short are the yards of a ship,)
uneasy are autumn nights;
Full oft does the weather change in a week,
and more in a month's time.
BELLOWS

* See publishers note at beginning of book.

75. Veit-a hinn,
er vettki veit,
margr verðr af aurum api;
maðr er auðigr,
annar óauðigr,
skyli-t þann vítka váar.

74. He that learns nought will never know
how one is the fool of another,
for if one be rich another is poor
and for that should bear no blame.
BRAY

75. He (only) knows not
who knows nothing,
that many a one apes another.
One man is rich, another poor:
let him not be thought blameworthy.
THORPE

75. A man knows not, if nothing he knows,
that gold oft apes begets;
One man is wealthy and one is poor,
yet scorn for him none should know.
BELLOWS

76. Deyr fé,
deyja frændr,
deyr sjalfr it sama,
en orðstírr
deyr aldregi,
hveim er sér góðan getr.

75. Cattle die and kinsmen die,
thyself too soon must die,
but one thing never, I ween, will die,
fair fame of one who has earned.
BRAY

76. Cattle die,
kindred die,
we ourselves also die;
but the fair fame never dies
of him who has earned it.
THORPE

77. Cattle die, and kinsmen die,
and so one dies one's self;
But a noble name will never die,
if good renown one gets.
BELLOWS

77. Deyr fé,
deyja frændr,
deyr sjalfr it sama,
ek veit einn,
at aldrei deyr:
dómr um dauðan hvern.

76. Cattle die and kinsmen die,
thyself too soon must die,
but one thing never, I ween, will die,
the doom on each one dead.
BRAY

77. Cattle die,
kindred die,
we ourselves also die;
but I know one thing
that never dies,
judgement on each one dead.
THORPE

78. Cattle die, and kinsmen die,
and so one dies one's self;
One thing I know that never dies,
the fame of a dead man's deeds.
BELLOWS

78. Fullar grindr
sá ek fyr Fitjungs sonum,
nú bera þeir vánar völ;
svá er auðr
sem augabragð,
hann er valtastr vina.

77. Full-stocked folds had the Fatling's sons,
who bear now a beggar's staff:
brief is wealth, as the winking of an eye,
most faithless ever of friends.
BRAY

78. Full storehouses I saw
at Dives' sons':
now bear they the beggar's staff.
Such are riches;
as is the twinkling of an eye:
of friends they are most fickle.
THORPE

76. Among Fitjung's sons
saw I well-stocked folds,
now bear they the beggar's staff;
Wealth is as swift as a winking eye,
of friends the falsest it is.
BELLOWS

79. Ósnotr maðr,
ef eignask getr
fé eða fljóðs munuð,
metnaðr hánum þróask,
en mannvit aldregi,
fram gengr hann drjúgt í dul.

78. If haply a fool should find for himself
wealth or a woman's love,
pride waxes in him but wisdom never
and onward he fares in his folly.
BRAY

79. A foolish man,
if he acquires wealth
or a woman's love,
pride grows within him,
but wisdom never:
he goes on more and more arrogant.
THORPE

80. An unwise man,
if a maiden's love or wealth he chances to win;
His pride will wax, but his wisdom never,
straight forward he fares in conceit.
BELLOWS

80. Þat er þá reynt,
er þú að rúnum spyrr
inum reginkunnum,
þeim er gerðu ginnregin
ok fáði fimbulþulr,
þá hefir hann bazt, ef hann þegir.

79. All will prove true
that thou askest of runes
those that are come from the gods,
which the high Powers wrought,
and which Odin painted:
then silence is surely best.
BRAY

80. Then 'tis made manifest,
if of runes thou questionest him,
those to the high ones known,
which the great powers invented,
and the great talker painted,
that he had best hold silence.
THORPE

79. Certain is that which
is sought from runes,
that the Gods so great have made,
and the Master-Poet painted,
of the race of Gods;
Silence is safest and best.
BELLOWS

81. At kveldi skal dag leyfa,
konu, er brennd er,
mæki, er reyndr er,
mey, er gefin er,
ís, er yfir kemr,
öl, er drukkit er.

80. Praise day at even, a wife when dead,
a weapon when tried, a maid when married,
ice when 'tis crossed, and ale when 'tis drunk.
BRAY

81. At eve the day is to be praised,
a woman after she is burnt,
a sword after it is proved,
a maid after she is married,
ice after it has passed away,
beer after it is drunk.
THORPE

81. Give praise to the day at evening,
to a woman on her pyre,
to a weapon which is tried,
to a maid at wed-lock,
to ice when it is crossed,
to ale that is drunk.
BELLOWS

82. Í vindi skal við höggva,
veðri á sjó róa,
myrkri við man spjalla,
mörg eru dags augu;
á skip skal skriðar orka,
en á skjöld til hlífar,
mæki höggs,
en mey til kossa.

81. Hew wood in wind,
sail the seas in a breeze,
woo a maid in the dark,
for day's eyes are many,
work a ship for its gliding,
a shield for its shelter,
a sword for its striking,
a maid for her kiss;
BRAY

82. In the wind one should hew wood,
in a breeze row out to sea,
in the dark talk with a lass:
many are the eyes of day.
In a ship voyages are to be made,
but a shield is for protection,
a sword for striking,
but a damsel for a kiss.
THORPE

82. When the gale blows hew wood,
in fair winds seek the water;
Sport with maidens at dusk,
for day's eyes are many;
From the ship seek swiftness,
from the shield protection,
cuts from the sword,
from the maiden kisses.
BELLOWS

83. Við eld skal öl drekka,
en á ísi skríða,
magran mar kaupa,
en mæki saurgan,
heima hest feita,
en hund á búi.

82. Drink ale by the fire,
but slide on the ice;
buy a steed when 'tis lanky,
a sword when 'tis rusty;
feed thy horse neath a roof,
and thy hound in the yard.
BRAY

83. By the fire one should drink beer,
on the ice slide;
but a horse that is lean,
a sword that is rusty;
feed a horse at home,
but a dog at the farm.
THORPE

83. By the fire drink ale,
over ice go on skates;
Buy a steed that is lean,
and a sword when tarnished;
The horse at home fatten,
the hound in thy dwelling.
BELLOWS

84. Meyjar orðum
skyli manngi trúa
né því, er kveðr kona,
því at á hverfanda hvéli
váru þeim hjörtu sköpuð,
brigð í brjóst of lagið.

83. The speech of a maiden,
should no man trust
nor the words which a woman says;
for their hearts were shaped,
on a whirling wheel,
and falsehood fixed in their breasts.
BRAY

84. In a maiden's words
no one should place faith,
nor in what a woman says;
for on a turning wheel
have their hearts been formed,
and guile in their breasts been laid;
THORPE

84. A man shall trust not,
the oath of a maid,
nor the word a woman speaks;
For their hearts,
on a whirling wheel were fashioned,
and fickle their breasts were formed.
BELLOWS

85. Brestanda boga,
brennanda loga,
gínanda ulfi,
galandi kráku,
rýtanda svíni,
rótlausum viði,
vaxanda vági,
vellanda katli,

84. Breaking bow, or flaring flame,
ravening wolf, or croaking raven,
routing swine, or rootless tree,
waxing wave, or seething cauldron,
BRAY

85. in a creaking bow, a burning flame,
a yawning wolf, a chattering crow,
a grunting swine, a rootless tree,
a waxing wave, a boiling kettle,
THORPE

85. In a breaking bow or a burning flame,
a ravening wolf or a croaking raven;
In a grunting boar,
a tree with roots broken,
in billowy seas or a bubbling kettle,
BELLOWS

86. Fljúganda fleini,
fallandi báru,
ísi einnættum,
ormi hringlegnum,
brúðar beðmálum
eða brotnu sverði,
bjarnar leiki
eða barni konungs.

85. flying arrows, or falling billow,
ice of a nighttime, coiling adder,
woman's bed-talk, or broken blade,
play of bears or a prince's child,
BRAY

86. a flying dart,
a falling billow,
a one night's ice,
a coiled serpent,
a woman's bed-talk,
or a broken sword,
a bear's play,
or a royal child,
THORPE

86. In a flying arrow or falling waters,
in ice new formed or the serpent's folds,
in a bride's bed-speech or a broken sword,
in the sport of bears or in sons of kings
BELLOWS

87. sjúkum kálfi
sjálfráða þræli
völu vilmæli
val nýfeldum

86.
sickly calf or self-willed thrall,
witch's flattery, new-slain foe,
BRAY

87. a sick calf,
a self-willed thrall,
a flattering prophetess,
a corpse newly slain,
(a serene sky,
a laughing lord,
a barking dog,
and a harlot's grief);
THORPE

87. In a calf that is sick or a stubborn thrall,
a flattering witch or a foe new slain,
in a light, clear sky or a laughing throng,
in the howl of a dog or a harlot's grief.
BELLOWS

88. Akri ársánum
trúi engi maðr
né til snemma syni,
- veðr ræðr akri.
en vit syni;
hætt er þeira hvárt.

87. Let none put faith in the first sown fruit
nor yet in his son too soon;
whim rules the child, and weather the field,
each is open to chance.
BRAY

88. an early sown field
let no one trust,
nor prematurely in a son:
weather rules the field,
and wit the son,
each of which is doubtful;
THORPE

89. Hope not too surely for early harvest,
nor trust too soon in thy son;
The field needs good weather,
the son needs wisdom,
and oft is either denied.
BELLOWS

89. Bróðurbana sínum
þótt á brautu mæti,
húsi hálfbrunnu,
hesti alskjótum,
þá er jór ónýtr,
ef einn fótr brotnar,
verði-t maðr svá tryggr
at þessu trúi öllu.

86.(con) brother's slayer,
though seen on the highway,
half burned house, or horse too swift
be never so trustful as these to trust.
BRAY

89. a brother's murderer,
though on the high road met,
a half-burnt house, an over-swift horse,
(a horse is useless, if a leg be broken),
no man is so confiding as to trust any of these.
THORPE

88. In a brother's slayer,
if thou meet him abroad,
in a half-burned house,
in a horse full swift,
one leg is hurt and the horse is useless;
None had ever such faith
as to trust in them all.
BELLOWS

90. Svá er friðr kvenna,
þeira er flátt hyggja,
sem aki jó óbryddum
á ísi hálum,
teitum, tvévetrum
ok sé tamr illa,
eða í byr óðum
beiti stjórnlausu,
eða skyli haltr henda
hrein í þáfjalli.

88. Like the love of women,
whose thoughts are lies,
is the driving un-roughshod,
o'er slippery ice of a two year old,
ill-tamed and gay;
or in a wild wind,
steering a helmless ship,
or the lame catching,
reindeer in the rime-thawed fell.
BRAY

90. Such is the love of women,
who falsehood meditate,
as if one drove not rough-shod,
on slippery ice,
a spirited two-years old
and unbroken horse;
or as in a raging storm
a helmless ship is beaten;
or as if the halt were set to catch
a reindeer in the thawing fell.
THORPE

90. The love of women fickle of will,
is like starting o'er ice with a steed unshod,
a two-year-old restive and little tamed,
or steering a rudderless ship in a storm,
or lame, hunting reindeer on slippery rocks.
BELLOWS

91. Bert ek nú mæli,
því at ek bæði veit,
brigðr er karla hugr konum;
þá vér fegrst mælum,
er vér flást hyggjum:
þat tælir horska hugi.

89. Now plainly I speak,
since both I have seen;
unfaithful is man to maid;
we speak them fairest when
thoughts are falsest and
wile the wisest of hearts.
BRAY

91. Openly I now speak,
because I both sexes know:
unstable are men's minds towards women;
'tis then we speak most fair
when we most falsely think:
that deceives even the cautious.
THORPE

91. Clear now will I speak,
for I know them both;
Men false to women are found,
when fairest we speak, then falsest we think;
Against wisdom we work with deceit.
BELLOWS

92. Fagrt skal mæla
ok fé bjóða,
sá er vill fljóðs ást fá,
líki leyfa
ins ljósa mans,
sá fær, er fríar.

90. Let him speak soft words
and offer wealth
who longs for a woman's love,
praise the shape of the shining maid,
he wins who thus doth woo.
BRAY

92. Fair shall speak,
and money offer,
who would obtain a woman's love.
Praise the form
of a fair damsel;
he gets who courts her.
THORPE

92. Soft words shall he speak,
and wealth shall he offer
who longs for a maiden's love;
And the beauty praise of the maiden bright,
he wins whose wooing is best.
BELLOWS

93. Ástar firna
skyli engi maðr
annan aldregi;
oft fá á horskan,
er á heimskan né fá,
lostfagrir litir.

91. Never a whit should one blame another
whom love hath brought into bonds:
oft a witching form will fetch the wise
which holds not the heart of fools.
BRAY

93. At love should no one
ever wonder in another:
a beauteous countenance
oft captivates the wise,
which captivates not the foolish.
THORPE

93. Fault for loving
let no man find ever with any other;
Oft the wise are fettered,
where fools go free,
by beauty that breeds desire.
BELLOWS

94. Eyvitar firna
er maðr annan skal,
þess er um margan gengr guma;
heimska ór horskum
gerir hölða sonu
sá inn máttki munr.

92. Never a whit should one blame another
for a folly which many befalls;
the might of love makes sons of men
into fools who once were wise.
BRAY

94. Let no one wonder at
another's folly,
it is the lot of many.
All-powerful desire
makes of the sons of men
fools even of the wise.
THORPE

94. Fault with another let no man find,
for what touches many a man;
Wise men oft into witless fools,
are made by mighty love.
BELLOWS

95. Hugr einn þat veit,
er býr hjarta nær,
einn er hann sér of sefa;
öng er sótt verri
hveim snotrum manni
en sér engu at una.

93. The mind knows alone
what is nearest the heart
and sees where the soul is turned:
no sickness seems to the wise so sore
as in nought to know content.
BRAY

95. The mind only knows
what lies near the heart,
that alone is conscious of our affections.
No disease is worse to a sensible man
than not to be content with himself.
THORPE

95. The head alone knows
what dwells near the heart,
a man knows his mind alone;
No sickness is worse to one who is wise,
than to lack the longed-for joy.
BELLOWS

96. Þat ek þá reynda,
er ek í reyri sat,
ok væ ttak míns munar;
hold ok hjarta
var mér in horska mær;
þeygi ek hana at heldr hefik.

94. This once I felt when I sat without
in the reeds, and looked for my love;
body and soul of me was that sweet maiden
yet never I won her as wife.
BRAY

96. That I experienced,
when in the reeds I sat,
awaiting my delight.
Body and soul to me
was that discreet maiden:
nevertheless I posses her not.
THORPE

96. This found I myself,
when I sat in the reeds,
and long my love awaited;
As my life the maiden wise I loved,
yet her I never had.
BELLOWS

97. Billings mey
ek fann beðjum á
sólhvíta sofa;
jarls yndi
þótti mér ekki vera
nema við þat lík at lifa.

95. Billing's daughter I found on her bed,
fairer than sunlight sleeping,
and the sweets of lordship seemed to me
nought, save I lived with that lovely form.
BRAY

97. Billing's lass
on her couch I found,
sun-bright, sleeping.
A prince's joy
to me seemed naught,
if not with that form to live.
THORPE

97. Billing's daughter I found on her bed,
in slumber bright as the sun;
Empty appeared an earl's estate,
without that form so fair.
BELLOWS

98. "Auk nær aftni
skaltu, Óðinn, koma,
ef þú vilt þér mæla man;
allt eru ósköp,
nema einir viti
slíkan löst saman."

96. "Yet nearer evening come thou,
Odin, if thou wilt woo a maiden:
all were undone save two knew alone
such a secret deed of shame."
BRAY

98. "Yet nearer eve
must thou, Odin, come,
if thou wilt talk the maiden over;
all will be disastrous,
unless we alone
are privy to such misdeed."
THORPE

98. "Odin, again at evening come,
if a woman thou wouldst win;
Evil it were if others than we,
should know of such a sin."
BELLOWS

99. Aftr ek hvarf
ok unna þóttumk
vísum vilja frá;
hitt ek hugða,
at ek hafa mynda
geð hennar allt ok gaman.

97. So away I turned from my wise intent,
and deemed my joy assured,
for all her liking and all her love
I weened that I yet should win.
BRAY

99. I returned,
thinking to love,
at her wise desire.
I thought
I should obtain
her whole heart and love.
THORPE

99. Away I hastened,
hoping for joy,
and careless of counsel wise;
Well I believed that soon,
I should win measureless joy with the maid.
BELLOWS

100. Svá kom ek næst,
at in nýta var
vígdrótt öll of vakin
með brennandum ljósum
ok bornum viði,
svá var mér vílstígr of vitaðr.

98. When I came ere long
the war troop bold
were watching and waking all:
with burning brands and torches borne
they showed me my sorrowful way.
BRAY

100. When next I came
the bold warriors were
all awake,
with lights burning,
and bearing torches:
thus was the way to pleasure closed.
THORPE

100. So came I next when night it was,
The warriors all were awake;
With burning lights,
and waving brands,
I learned my luckless way.
BELLOWS

101. Ok nær morni
er ek var enn um kominn
þá var saldrótt um sofin
grey eitt ek þá fann
innar góðu konu
bundit beðjum á

99. Yet nearer morning I went, once more,
the housefolk slept in the hall,
but soon I found a barking dog
tied fast to that fair maid's couch.
BRAY

101. But at the approach of morn,
when again I came,
the household all was sleeping;
the good damsel's dog
alone I found
tied to the bed.
THORPE

101. At morning then,
when once more I came,
and all were sleeping still,
a dog I found in the fair one's place;
Bound there upon her bed.
BELLOWS

102. Mörg er góð mær,
ef görva kannar,
hugbrigð við hali;
þá ek þat reynda,
er it ráðspaka
teygða ek á flærðir fljóð;
háðungar hverrar
leitaði mér it horska man,
ok hafða ek þess vettki vífs.

100. Many a sweet maid
when one knows her mind
is fickle found towards men:
I proved it well when that prudent lass
I sought to lead astray:
shrewd maid, she sought me with every insult
and I won therewith no wife.
BRAY

102. Many a fair maiden,
when rightly known,
towards men is fickle:
that I experienced,
when that discreet maiden I
strove to seduce:
contumely of every kind
that wily girl
heaped upon me;
nor of that damsel gained I aught.
THORPE

102. Many fair maids,
if a man but tries them,
false to a lover are found;
That did I learn,
when I longed to gain
with wiles the maiden wise;
Foul scorn was my meed from the crafty maid,
And naught from the woman I won.
BELLOWS

103. Heima glaðr gumi
ok við gesti reifr,
sviðr skal um sig vera,
minnigr ok málugr,
ef hann vill margfróðr vera,
oft skal góðs geta;
fimbulfambi heitir,
sá er fátt kann segja,
þat er ósnotrs aðal.

101. In thy home be joyous,
and generous to guests
discreet shalt thou be in thy bearing,
mindful and talkative,
wouldst thou gain wisdom,
oft making me mention of good.
He is "Simpleton" named,
who has nought to say,
for such is the fashion of fools.
BRAY

103. At home let a man be cheerful,
and towards a guest liberal;
of wise conduct he should be,
of good memory and ready speech;
if much knowledge he desires,
he must often talk on good.

----

104. Fimbulfambi he is called
who little has to say:
such is the nature of the simple.
THORPE

103. Though glad at home,
and merry with guests,
a man shall be wary and wise;
The sage and shrewd,
wide wisdom seeking,
must see that his speech be fair;
A fool is he named who naught can say,
for such is the way of the witless.
BELLOWS

104. Inn aldna jötun ek sótta,
nú em ek aftr of kominn:
fátt gat ek þegjandi þar;
mörgum orðum
mælta ek í minn frama
í Suttungs sölum.

102. I sought that old Jötun,
now safe am I back,
little served my silence there;
but whispering many soft speeches I won
my desire in Suttung's halls.
BRAY

105. The old Jötun I sought;
now I am come back:
little got I there by silence;
in many words
I spoke to my advantage
in Suttung's halls.
THORPE

104. I found the old giant,
now back have I fared,
small gain from silence I got;
Full many a word, my will to get,
I spoke in Suttung's hall.
BELLOWS

105. Gunnlöð mér of gaf
gullnum stóli á
drykk ins dýra mjaðar;
ill iðgjöld
lét ek hana eftir hafa
síns ins heila hugar,
síns ins svára sefa.

104. 'Twas Gunnlod
who gave me on a golden throne
a draught of the glorious mead,
but with poor reward did I pay her back
for her true and troubled heart.
BRAY

106. Gunnlöd gave me,
on her golden seat,
a draught of the precious mead;
a bad recompense
I afterwards made her,
for her whole soul,
her fervent love.
THORPE

106. Gunnlod gave on a golden stool,
a drink of the marvelous mead;
A harsh reward did I let her have,
for her heroic heart,
and her spirit troubled sore.
BELLOWS

106. Rata munn
létumk rúms of fá
ok um grjót gnaga;
yfir ok undir
stóðumk jötna vegir,
svá hætta ek höfði til.

103. I bored me a road there with Rati's tusk
and made room to pass through the rock;
while the ways of the Jötuns
stretched over and under,
I dared my life for a draught.
BRAY

107. Rati's mouth I caused
to make a space,
and to gnaw the rock;
over and under me
were the Jötun's ways:
thus I my head did peril.
THORPE

105. The mouth of Rati,
made room for my passage,
and space in the stone he gnawed;
Above and below the giants' paths lay,
so rashly I risked my head.
BELLOWS

107. Vel keypts litar
hefi ek vel notit,
fás er fróðum vant,
því at Óðrerir
er nú upp kominn
á alda vés jaðar.

105. In a wily disguise I worked my will;
little is lacking to the wise,
for the Soul-stirrer now,
sweet Mead of Song,
is brought to men's earthly abode.
BRAY

108. Of a well-assumed form
I made good use:
few things fail the wise;
for Odhrærir
is now come up
to men's earthly dwellings.
THORPE

107. The well-earned beauty well I enjoyed,
little the wise man lacks;
So Othrorir now has up been brought,
to the midst of the men of earth.
BELLOWS

108. Ifi er mér á,
at ek væra enn kominn
jötna görðum ór,
ef ek Gunnlaðar né nytak,
innar góðu konu,
þeirar er lögðumk arm yfir.

106. I misdoubt me if ever again I had come
from the realms of the Jötun race,
had I not served me of Gunnlod,
sweet woman,
her whom I held in mine arms.
BRAY

109. 'Tis to me doubtful
that I could have come
from the Jötun's courts,
had not Gunnlöd aided me,
that good damsel,
over whom I laid my arm.
THORPE

108. Hardly, methinks,
would I home have come,
and left the giants' land,
had not Gunnloth helped me,
the maiden good,
whose arms about me had been.
BELLOWS

109. Ins hindra dags
gengu hrímþursar
Háva ráðs at fregna
Háva höllu í;
at Bölverki þeir spurðu,
ef hann væri með böndum kominn
eða hefði hánum Suttungr of sóit.

107. Came forth, next day,
the dread Frost Giants,
and entered the High One's Hall:
they asked,
was the Baleworker back mid the Powers,
or had Suttung slain him below?
BRAY

110. On the day following
came the Hrim-thursar,
to learn something of the High One,
in the High One's hall:
after Bölverk they inquired,
whether he with the gods were come,
or Suttung had destroyed him?
THORPE

109. The day that followed,
the frost-giants came;
Some word of Hor to win,
(and into the hall of Hor;)
of Bolverk they asked,
were he back midst the gods,
or had Suttung slain him there?
BELLOWS

* Bolverk, Bölverk, Baleworker (Evil Doer)

110. Baugeið Óðinn,
hygg ek, at unnit hafi;
hvat skal hans tryggðum trúa?
Suttung svikinn
hann lét sumbli frá
ok grætta Gunnlöðu.

108. A ring-oath Odin I trow had taken,
how shall one trust his troth?
'twas he who stole the mead from Suttung,
and Gunnlod caused to weep.
BRAY

111. Odin, I believe,
a ring-oath gave.
Who in his faith will trust?
Suttung defrauded,
of his drink bereft,
and Gunnlöd made to weep!
THORPE

110. On his ring swore Odin the oath, methinks;
Who now his troth shall trust?
Suttung's betrayal he sought with drink,
and Gunnloth to grief he left.
BELLOWS

111. Mál er at þylja
þular stóli á
Urðarbrunni at,
sá ek ok þagðak,
sá ek ok hugðak,
hlýdda ek á manna mál;
of rúnar heyrða ek dæma,
né of ráðum þögðu
Háva höllu at,
Háva höllu í,
heyrða ek segja svá:

109. 'Tis time to speak
from the Sage's Seat;
hard by the Well of Weird
I saw and was silent, I saw and pondered,
I listened to the speech of men.
BRAY

110. Of runes they spoke,
and the reading of runes
was little withheld from their lips:
at the High One's hall,
in the High One's hall,
I thus heard the High One say:
BRAY

112. Time 'tis to discourse
from the preacher's chair. -
By the well of Urd
I silent sat,
I saw and meditated,
I listened to men's words.
THORPE

113. Of runes I heard discourse,
and of things divine,
nor of graving them were they silent,
nor of sage counsels,
at the High One's hall.
In the High One's hall.
I thus heard say:
THORPE

111. It is time to chant
from the chanter's stool;
By the wells of Urth I was,
I saw and was silent,
I saw and thought,
and heard the speech of Hon
of runes heard I words,
nor were counsel wanting;
At the hall of Hor;
In the hall of Hor;
Such was the speech I heard.)
BELLOWS

112. Ráðumk þér, Loddfáfnir,
en þú ráð nemir, -
njóta mundu, ef þú nemr,
þér munu góð, ef þú getr -:
nótt þú rísat
nema á njósn séir
eða þú leitir þér innan út staðar.

111. I counsel thee, Stray-Singer,
accept my counsels,
they will be thy boon if thou obey'st them,
they will work thy weal if thou win'st them:
rise never at nighttime, except thou art spying
or seekest a spot without.
BRAY

114. I counsel thee, Loddfafnir,
to take advise:
thou wilt profit if thou takest it.
Rise not a night, unless to explore,
or art compelled to go out.
THORPE

112. I rede thee, Loddfafnir!
and hear thou my rede,
Profit thou hast if thou hearest,
Great thy gain if thou learnest:
Rise not at night, save if news thou seekest,
Or fain to the outhouse wouldst fare.
BELLOWS

113. Ráðumk þér, Loddfáfnir,
en þú ráð nemir, -
njóta mundu, ef þú nemr,
þér munu góð, ef þú getr -:
fjölkunnigri konu
skal-at-tu í faðmi sofa,
svá at hon lyki þik liðum.

112. I counsel thee, Stray-Singer,
accept my counsels,
they will be thy boon
if thou obey'st them,
they will work thy weal
if thou win'st them:
thou shalt never sleep
in the arms of a sorceress,
lest she should lock thy limbs;
BRAY

115. I counsel thee, Loddfafnir,
to take advice,
thou wilt profit if thou takest it.
In an enchantress's embrace
thou mayest not sleep,
so that in her arms she clasp thee.
THORPE

113. I rede thee, Loddfafnir!
and hear thou my rede,
Profit thou hast if thou hearest,
Great thy gain if thou learnest:
Beware of sleep on a witch's bosom,
Nor let her limbs ensnare thee.
BELLOWS

114. Hon svá gørir
at þú gáir eigi
þings né þjóðans máls
mat þú villat
né mannskis gaman
ferr þú sorgafullr at sofa

113. So shall she charm,
that thou shalt not heed
the council, or words of the king,
nor care for thy food,
or the joys of mankind,
but fall into sorrowful sleep.
BRAY

116. She will be the cause
that thou carest not
for Thing or prince's words;
food thou wilt shun
and human joys;
sorrowful wilt thou go to sleep.
THORPE

114. Such is her might,
that thou hast no mind,
for the council or meeting of men;
Meat thou hatest,
joy thou hast not,
and sadly to slumber thou farest.
BELLOWS

115. Ráðumk þér, Loddfáfnir,
en þú ráð nemir, -
njóta mundu, ef þú nemr,
þér munu góð, ef þú getr -:
annars konu
teygðu þér aldregi
eyrarúnu at.

114. I counsel thee, Stray-Singer,
accept my counsels,
they will be thy boon if thou obey'st them,
they will work thy weal if thou win'st them:
seek not ever to draw to thyself
in love-whispering another's wife.
BRAY

117. I counsel thee, Loddfafnir,
to take advice,
thou wilt profit if thou takest it.
Another's wife entice thou never
to secret converse.
THORPE

115. I rede thee, Loddfafnir!
and hear thou my rede,
Profit thou hast if thou hearest,
Great thy gain if thou learnest:
Seek never to win the wife of another,
or long for her secret love.
BELLOWS

116. Ráðumk þér, Loddfáfnir,
en þú ráð nemir,
njóta mundu, ef þú nemr,
þér munu góð, ef þú getr -:
á fjalli eða firði,
ef þik fara tíðir,
fásktu at virði vel.

115. I counsel thee, Stray-Singer,
accept my counsels,
they will be thy boon if thou obey'st them,
they will work thy weal if thou win'st them:
should thou long to fare over fell and firth
provide thee well with food.
BRAY

118. I counsel thee, Loddfafnir,
to take advice,
thou wilt profit if thou takest it.
By fell or firth if thou have to travel,
provide thee well with food.
THORPE

116. I rede thee, Loddfafnir!
and hear thou my rede,
Profit thou hast if thou hearest,
Great thy gain if thou learnest:
If o'er mountains or gulfs thou fain wouldst
go, look well to thy food for the way.
BELLOWS

117. Ráðumk þér, Loddfáfnir,
en þú ráð nemir,
njóta mundu, ef þú nemr,
þér munu góð, ef þú getr -:
illan mann
láttu aldregi
óhöpp at þér vita,
því at af illum manni
fær þú aldregi
gjöld ins góða hugar.

116. I counsel thee, Stray-Singer,
accept my counsels,
they will be thy boon if thou obey'st them,
they will work thy weal if thou win'st them:
tell not ever an evil man
if misfortunes thee befall,
from such ill friend thou needst never seek
return for thy trustful mind.
BRAY

119. I counsel thee, Loddfafnir,
to take advice,
thou wilt profit if thou takest it.
A bad man let thou never
know thy misfortunes;
for from a bad man
thou never wilt obtain
a return for thy good will.
THORPE

117. I rede thee, Loddfafnir!
and hear thou my rede,
Profit thou hast if thou hearest,
Great thy gain if thou learnest:
An evil man thou must not let bring,
aught of ill to thee;
For an evil man,
will never make reward for a worthy thought.
BELLOWS

118. Ofarla bíta
ek sá einum hal
orð illrar konu;
fláráð tunga
varð hánum at fjörlagi
ok þeygi of sanna sök.

117. Wounded to death, have I seen a man
by the words of an evil woman;
a lying tongue had bereft him of life,
and all without reason of right.
BRAY

120. I saw mortally
wound a man
a wicked woman's words;
a false tongue
caused his death,
and most unrighteously.
THORPE

118. I saw a man,
who was wounded sore,
by an evil woman's word;
A lying tongue his death-blow launched,
and no word of truth there was.
BELLOWS

119. Ráðumk þér, Loddfáfnir,
en þú ráð nemir, -
njóta mundu, ef þú nemr,
þér munu góð, ef þú getr -:
veistu, ef þú vin átt,
þann er þú vel trúir,
far þú at finna oft,
því at hrísi vex
ok hávu grasi
vegr, er vættki treðr.

118. I counsel thee, Stray-Singer,
accept my counsels,
they will be thy boon if thou obey'st them,
they will work thy weal if thou win'st them:
hast thou a friend whom thou trustest well,
fare thou to find him oft;
for with brushwood grows and with grasses
high the path where no foot doth pass.
BRAY

121. I counsel thee, Loddfafnir,
to take advice,
thou wilt profit if thou takest it.
If thou knowest thou has a friend,
whom thou well canst trust,
go oft to visit him; for with brushwood over-
grown, and with high grass,
is the way that no one treads.
THORPE

119. I rede thee, Loddfafnir!
and hear thou my rede,
Profit thou hast if thou hearest,
Great thy gain if thou learnest:
If a friend thou hast,
whom thou fully wilt trust,
then fare to find him oft;
For brambles grow and waving grass,
on the rarely trodden road.
BELLOWS

120. Ráðumk þér, Loddfáfnir,
en þú ráð nemir,
njóta mundu, ef þú nemr,
þér munu góð, ef þú getr -:
góðan mann
teygðu þér at gamanrúnum
ok nem líknargaldr, meðan þú lifir.

119. I counsel thee, Stray-Singer,
accept my counsels,
they will be thy boon if thou obey'st them,
they will work thy weal if thou win'st them:
in sweet converse call the righteous to thy side,
learn a healing song while thou livest.
BRAY

122. I counsel thee, Loddfafnir,
to take advice,
thou wilt profit if thou takest it.
A good man attract to thee
in pleasant converse;
and salutary speech learn while thou livest.
THORPE

120. I rede thee, Loddfafnir!
and hear thou my rede,
Profit thou hast if thou hearest,
Great thy gain if thou learnest:
A good man find to hold in friendship,
and give heed to his healing charms.
BELLOWS

121. Ráðumk þér, Loddfáfnir,
en þú ráð nemir,
njóta mundu, ef þú nemr,
þér munu góð, ef þú getr -:
vin þínum
ver þú aldregi
fyrri at flaumslitum;
sorg etr hjarta,
ef þú segja né náir
einhverjum allan hug.

120. I counsel thee, Stray-Singer,
accept my counsels,
they will be thy boon if thou obey'st them,
they will work thy weal if thou win'st them:
be never the first with friend of thine
to break the bond of fellowship;
care shall gnaw thy heart if thou canst not tell
all thy mind to another.
BRAY

123. I counsel thee, Loddfafnir,
to take advice,
thou wilt profit if thou takest it.
With thy friend be thou never
first to quarrel.
Care gnaws the heart,
if thou to no one canst
thy whole mind disclose.
THORPE

121. I rede thee, Loddfafnir! and hear thou my rede,
Profit thou hast if thou hearest,
Great thy gain if thou learnest:
Be never the first to break with thy friend,
the bond that holds you both;
Care eats the heart,
if thou canst not speak to another all thy thought.
BELLOWS

122. Ráðumk þér, Loddfáfnir,
en þú ráð nemir,
njóta mundu, ef þú nemr,
þér munu góð, ef þú getr -:
orðum skipta
þú skalt aldregi
við ósvinna apa,

121. I counsel thee, Stray-Singer,
accept my counsels,
they will be thy boon if thou obey'st them,
they will work thy weal if thou win'st them:
never in speech with a foolish knave
shouldst thou waste a single word.
BRAY

124. I counsel thee, Loddfafnir,
to take advice,
thou wilt profit if thou takest it.
Words thou never shouldst exchange
with a witless fool;
THORPE

122. I rede thee, Loddfafnir!
and hear thou my rede,
Profit thou hast if thou hearest,
Great thy gain if thou learnest:
Exchange of words with a witless ape
Thou must not ever make.
BELLOWS

123. Því at af illum manni
mundu aldregi
góðs laun um geta,
en góðr maðr
mun þik gerva mega
líknfastan at lofi.

122. From the lips of such
thou needst not look
for reward of thine own good will;
but a righteous man
by praise will render thee
firm in favour and love.
BRAY

125. for from an ill-conditioned man
thou wilt never get
a return for good;
but a good man will
bring thee favour
by his praise.
THORPE

123. For never thou mayst,
from an evil man a good requital get;
But a good man oft the greatest love,
through words of praise will win thee.
BELLOWS

124. Sifjum er þá blandat,
hver er segja ræðr
einum allan hug;
allt er betra
en sé brigðum at vera;
era sá vinr öðrum,
er vilt eitt segir.

123. There is mingling in friendship,
when man can utter
all his whole mind to another;
there is nought so vile as a fickle tongue;
no friend is he who but flatters.
BRAY

126. There is a mingling of affection,
where one can tell
another all his mind.
Everything is better
than being with the deceitful.
He is not another's friend
who ever says as he says.
THORPE

124. There is mingled affection,
when a man can speak to another all his thought;
Naught is so bad as false to be,
no friend speaks only fair.
BELLOWS

125. Ráðumk, þér Loddfáfnir,
en þú ráð nemir,
njóta mundu, ef þú nemr,
þér munu góð, ef þú getr -:
þrimr orðum senna
skalattu þér við verra mann
oft inn betri bilar,
þá er inn verri vegr.

124. I counsel thee, Stray-Singer,
accept my counsels,
they will be thy boon if thou obey'st them,
they will work thy weal if thou win'st them:
oft the worst lays the best one low.
BRAY

127. I counsel thee, Loddfafnir,
to take advice,
thou wilt profit if thou takest it.
Even in three words
quarrel not with a worse man:
often the better yields,
when the worse strikes.
THORPE

125. I rede thee, Loddfafnir!
and hear thou my rede,
Profit thou hast if thou hearest,
Great thy gain if thou learnest:
With a worse man
speak not three words in dispute,
Ill fares the better oft when the worse man
wields a sword.
BELLOWS

126. Ráðumk þér, Loddfáfnir,
en þú ráð nemir,
njóta mundu, ef þú nemr,
þér munu góð, ef þú getr -:
skósmiðr þú verir
né skeftismiðr,
nema þú sjalfum þér séir:
skór er skapaðr illa
eða skaft sé rangt,
þá er þér böls beðit.

125. I counsel thee, Stray-Singer,
accept my counsels,
they will be thy boon if thou obey'st them,
they will work thy weal if thou win'st them:
be not a shoemaker nor yet a shaft maker
save for thyself alone: let the shoe be
misshapen, or crooked the shaft, and a curse
on thy head will be called.
BRAY

128. I counsel thee, Loddfafnir,
to take advice,
thou wilt profit if thou takest it.
Be not a shoemaker, nor a shaftmaker,
unless for thyself it be; for a shoe if ill made,
or a shaft if crooked, will call down evil on
thee.
THORPE

126. I rede thee, Loddfafnir! and hear thou my rede,
Profit thou hast if thou hearest,
Great thy gain if thou learnest:
A shoemaker be,
or a maker of shafts,
for only thy single self;
If the shoe is ill made,
or the shaft prove false,
then evil of thee men think.
BELLOWS

127. Ráðumk þér, Loddfáfnir,
en þú ráð nemir,
njóta mundu, ef þú nemr,
þér munu góð, ef þú getr -:
hvars þú böl kannt,
kveð þú þér bölvi at
ok gefat þínum fjándum frið.

126. I counsel thee, Stray-Singer,
accept my counsels,
they will be thy boon if thou obey'st them,
they will work thy weal if thou win'st them:
when in peril thou seest thee, confess thee in
peril, nor ever give peace to thy foes.
BRAY

129. I counsel thee, Loddfafnir,
to take advice,
thou wilt profit if thou takest it.
Wherever of injury thou knowest,
regard that injury as thy own;
and give to thy foes no peace.
THORPE

127. I rede thee, Loddfafnir!
and hear thou my rede,
Profit thou hast if thou hearest,
Great thy gain if thou learnest:
If evil thou knowest, as evil proclaim it;
And make no friendship with foes.
BELLOWS

128. Ráðumk þér, Loddfáfnir,
en þú ráð nemir,
njóta mundu, ef þú nemr,
þér munu góð, ef þú getr -:
illu feginn
ver þú aldregi,
en lát þér at góðu getit.

127. I counsel thee, Stray-Singer,
accept my counsels,
they will be thy boon if thou obey'st them,
they will work thy weal if thou win'st them:
rejoice not ever at tidings of ill,
but glad let thy soul be in good.
BRAY

130. I counsel thee, Loddfafnir,
to take advice,
thou wilt profit if thou takest it
Rejoiced at evil be thou never;
but let good give thee pleasure.
THORPE

128. I rede thee, Loddfafnir!
and hear thou my rede,
Profit thou hast if thou hearest,
Great thy gain if thou learnest:
In evil never joy shalt thou know,
but glad the good shall make thee.
BELLOWS

129. Ráðumk þér, Loddfáfnir,
en þú ráð nemir, -
njóta mundu, ef þú nemr,
þér munu góð, ef þú getr
upp líta
skal-at-tu í orrustu,
gjalti glíkir
verða gumna synir,
síðr þitt of heilli halir.

128. I counsel thee, Stray-Singer,
accept my counsels,
they will be thy boon if thou obey'st them,
they will work thy weal if thou win'st them:
look not up in battle, when men are as beasts,
lest the wights bewitch thee with spells.
BRAY

131. I counsel thee, Loddfafnir,
to take advice,
thou wilt profit if thou takest it.
In a battle look not up,
(like swine the sons of men become)
that men may not fascinate thee.
THORPE

129. I rede thee, Loddfafnir!
and hear thou my rede,
Profit thou hast if thou hearest,
Great thy gain if thou learnest:
Look not up when the battle is on,
(Like madmen the sons of men become)
lest men bewitch thy wits.
BELLOWS

130. Ráðumk þér, Loddfáfnir,
en þú ráð nemir, -
njóta mundu, ef þú nemr,
þér munu góð, ef þú getr
ef þú vilt þér góða konu
kveðja at gamanrúnum
ok fá fögnuð af,
fögru skaltu heita
ok láta fast vera;
leiðisk manngi gótt, ef getr.

129. I counsel thee, Stray-Singer,
accept my counsels,
they will be thy boon if thou obey'st them,
they will work thy weal if thou win'st them:
wouldst thou win joy of a gentle maiden,
and lure to whispering of love,
thou shalt make fair promise,
and let it be fast,
none will scorn their weal who can win it.
BRAY

132. I counsel thee, Loddfafnir,
to take advice,
thou wilt profit if thou takest it.
If thou wilt induce a good woman
to pleasant converse, thou must promise fair,
and hold to it; no one turns from good if it
can be got.
THORPE

130. I rede thee, Loddfafnir!
and hear thou my rede,
Profit thou hast if thou hearest,
Great thy gain if thou learnest:
If thou fain wouldst win a woman's love,
and gladness get from her,
fair be thy promise and well fulfilled;
None loathes what good he gets.
BELLOWS

131. Ráðumk þér, Loddfáfnir,
en þú ráð nemir, -
njóta mundu, ef þú nemr,
þér munu góð, ef þú getr
varan bið ek þik vera
ok eigi ofvaran;
ver þú við öl varastr
ok við annars konu
ok við þat it þriðja,
at þjófar né leiki.

130. I counsel thee, Stray-Singer,
accept my counsels,
they will be thy boon if thou obey'st them,
they will work thy weal if thou win'st them:
I pray thee be wary, yet not too wary,
be wariest of all with ale,
with another's wife, and a third thing eke,
that knaves outwit thee never.
BRAY

133. I counsel thee, Loddfafnir,
to take advice,
thou wilt profit if thou takest it.
I enjoin thee to be wary,
but not over wary;
at drinking be thou most wary,
and with another's wife;
and thirdly, that thieves delude thee not.
THORPE

131. I rede thee, Loddfafnir!
and hear thou my rede,
Profit thou hast if thou hearest.
Great thy gain if thou learnest:
I bid thee be wary, but be not fearful;
(Beware most with ale or another's wife,
and third beware lest a thief outwit thee.)
BELLOWS

132. Ráðumk þér, Loddfáfnir,
en þú ráð nemir, -
njóta mundu, ef þú nemr,
þér munu góð, ef þú getr
at háði né hlátri
hafðu aldregi
gest né ganganda.

131. I counsel thee, Stray-Singer,
accept my counsels,
they will be thy boon if thou obey'st them,
they will work thy weal if thou win'st them:
hold not in scorn, nor mock in thy halls
a guest or wandering wight.
BRAY

134. I counsel thee, Loddfafnir,
to take advice,
thou wilt profit if thou takest it.
With insult or derision
treat thou never
a guest or wayfarer,
they often little know,
who sit within,
or what race they are who come.
THORPE

132. I rede thee, Loddfafnir!
and hear thou my rede,
Profit thou hast if thou hearest.
Great thy gain if thou learnest:
Scorn or mocking ne'er shalt thou make,
of a guest or a journey-goer.
BELLOWS

133. Oft vitu ógörla,
þeir er sitja inni fyrir,
hvers þeir ro kyns, er koma;
er-at maðr svá góðr
at galli né fylgi,
né svá illr, at einugi dugi.

132. They know but unsurely who sit within
what manner of man is come:
none is found so good,
but some fault attends him,
or so ill but he serves for somewhat.
BRAY

135. Vices and virtues
the sons of mortals bear
in their breasts mingled;
no one is so good
that no failing attends him,
nor so bad as to be good for nothing.
THORPE

133. Oft scarcely he knows,
who sits in the house,
what kind is the man who comes;
None so good is found that faults he has not,
nor so wicked that naught he is worth.
BELLOWS

134. Ráðumk þér, Loddfáfnir,
en þú ráð nemir, -
njóta mundu, ef þú nemr,
þér munu góð, ef þú getr -:
at hárum þul
hlæ þú aldregi,
oft er gótt, þat er gamlir kveða;
oft ór skörpum belg
skilin orð koma
þeim er hangir með hám
ok skollir með skrám
ok váfir með vílmögum

133. I counsel thee, Stray-Singer,
accept my counsels,
they will be thy boon if thou obey'st them,
they will work thy weal if thou win'st them:
hold never in scorn the hoary singer;
oft the counsel of the old is good;
come words of wisdom from the withered lips
of him left to hang among hides,
to rock with the rennets
and swing with the skins.
BRAY

136. I counsel thee, Loddfafnir,
to take advice,
thou wilt profit if thou takest it.
At a hoary speaker
laugh thou never;
often is good that which the aged utter,
oft from a shriveled hide
discreet words issue;
from those whose skin is pendent
and decked with scars,
and who go tottering among the vile.
THORPE

134. I rede thee, Loddfafnir!
and hear thou my rede,
Profit thou hast if thou hearest,
Great thy gain if thou learnest:
Scorn not ever the gray-haired singer,
oft do the old speak good;
(Oft from shriveled skin come skillful counsels,
though it hang with the hides,
and flap with the pelts,
and is blown with the bellies.)
BELLOWS

135. Ráðumk þér, Loddfáfnir,
en þú ráð nemir, -
njóta mundu, ef þú nemr,
þér munu góð, ef þú getr
gest þú né geyja
né á grind hrekir;
get þú váluðum vel.

134. I counsel thee, Stray-Singer,
accept my counsels,
they will be thy boon if thou obey'st them,
they will work thy weal if thou win'st them:
growl not at guests,
nor drive them from the gate
but show thyself gentle to the poor.
BRAY

137. I counsel thee, Loddfafnir,
to take advice,
thou wilt profit if thou takest it.
Rail not at a guest,
nor from thy gate thrust him;
treat well the indigent;
they will speak well of thee.
THORPE

135. I rede thee, Loddfafnir!
and hear thou my rede,
Profit thou hast if thou hearest,
Great thy gain if thou learnest:
Curse not thy guest, nor show him thy gate,
deal well with a man in want.
BELLOWS

136. Rammt er þat tré,
er ríða skal
öllum at upploki;
baug þú gef,
eða þat biðja mun
þér læs hvers á liðu.

135. Mighty is the bar to be moved away
for the entering in of all.
Shower thy wealth, or men shall wish thee
every ill in thy limbs.
BRAY

138. Strong is the bar
that must be raised
to admit all.
Do thou give a penny,
or they will call down on thee
every ill in thy limbs.
THORPE

136. Strong is the beam that raised,
must be to give an entrance to all;
Give it a ring,
or grim will be the wish,
it would work on thee.
BELLOWS

137. Ráðumk þér, Loddfáfnir,
en þú ráð nemir, -
njóta mundu, ef þú nemr,
þér munu góð, ef þú getr
hvars þú öl drekkir,
kjós þér jarðar megin,
því at jörð tekr við ölðri,
en eldr við sóttum,
eik við abbindi,
ax við fjölkynngi,
höll við hýrógi,
- heiftum skal mána kveðja, -
beiti við bitsóttum,
en við bölvi rúnar,
fold skal við flóði taka.

136. I counsel thee, Stray-Singer,
accept my counsels,
they will be thy boon if thou obey'st them,
they will work thy weal if thou win'st them:
when ale thou quaffest, call upon earth's
might, 'tis earth drinks in the floods.
Earth prevails o'er drink,
but fire o'er sickness,
the oak o'er binding,
the earcorn o'er witchcraft,
the rye spur o'er rupture,
the moon o'er rages,
herb o'er cattle plagues, runes o'er harm.
BRAY

139. I counsel thee, Loddfafnir,
to take advice,
thou wilt profit if thou takest it.
Wherever thou beer drinkest,
invoke to thee the power of earth;
for earth is good against drink,
fire for distempers,
the oak for constipation,
a corn-ear for sorcery
a hall for domestic strife.
In bitter hates invoke the moon;
the biter for bite-injuries is good;
but runes against calamity;
fluid let earth absorb.
THORPE

137. I rede thee, Loddfafnir!
and hear thou my rede,
Profit thou hast if thou hearest,
Great thy gain if thou learnest:
When ale thou drinkest, seek might of earth,
(For earth cures drink, and fire cures ills,
The oak cures tightness, the ear cures magic.
Rye cures rupture, the moon cures rage.
Grass cures the scab,
and runes the sword-cut;)
The field absorbs the flood.
BELLOWS

ODIN'S RUNE SONG

138. Veit ek, at ek hekk
vindga meiði á
nætr allar níu,
geiri undaðr
ok gefinn Óðni,
sjalfr sjalfum mér,
á þeim meiði,
er manngi veit
hvers af rótum renn.

137. I trow I hung on that windy Tree
nine whole days and nights,
stabbed with a spear, offered to Odin,
myself to mine own self given,
high on that Tree of which none hath heard
from what roots it rises to heaven.
BRAY

140. I know that I hung,
on a wind-rocked tree,
nine whole nights,
with a spear wounded,
and to Odin offered,
myself to myself;
on that tree,
of which no one knows
from what root it springs.
THORPE

139. I ween that I hung on the windy tree,
hung there for nights full nine;
With the spear I was wounded,
and offered I was to Odin,
myself to myself,
on the tree that none may ever know,
what root beneath it runs.
BELLOWS

139. Við hleifi mik sældu
né við hornigi;
nýsta ek niðr,
nam ek upp rúnar,
æpandi nam,
fell ek aftr þaðan.

138. None refreshed me ever with food or drink,
I peered right down in the deep;
crying aloud I lifted the Runes
then back I fell from thence.
BRAY

141. Bread no one gave me,
nor a horn of drink,
downward I peered,
to runes applied myself,
wailing learnt them,
then fell down thence.
THORPE

140. None made me happy
with loaf or horn,
and there below I looked;
I took up the runes,
shrieking I took them,
and forthwith back I fell.
BELLOWS

140. Fimbulljóð níu
nam ek af inum frægja syni
Bölþorns, Bestlu föður,
ok ek drykk of gat
ins dýra mjaðar,
ausinn Óðreri.

139. Nine mighty songs
I learned from the great
son of Bale-thorn, Bestla's sire;
I drank a measure of the wondrous Mead,
with the Soulstirrer's drops I was showered.
BRAY

142. Potent songs nine
from the famed son I learned
of Bölthorn, Bestla's sire,
and a draught obtained
of the precious mead,
drawn from Odhrærir.
THORPE

141. Nine mighty songs,
I got from the son of Bolthorn,
Bestla's father;
And a drink I got of the goodly mead,
poured out from Othrorir.
BELLOWS

141. Þá nam ek frævask
ok fróðr vera
ok vaxa ok vel hafask,
orð mér af orði
orðs leitaði,
verk mér af verki
verks leitaði.

140. Ere long I bare fruit, and throve full well,
I grew and waxed in wisdom;
word following word, I found me words,
deed following deed, I wrought deeds.
BRAY

143. Then I began to bear fruit,
and to know many things,
to grow and well thrive:
word by word
I sought out words,
fact by fact
I sought out facts.
THORPE

142. Then began I to thrive,
and wisdom to get,
I grew and well I was;
Each word led me on to another word,
each deed to another deed.
BELLOWS

142. Rúnar munt þú finna
ok ráðna stafi,
mjök stóra stafi,
mjök stinna stafi,
er fáði fimbulþulr
ok gerðu ginnregin
ok reist hroftr rögna.

141. Hidden Runes
shalt thou seek and interpreted signs,
many symbols of might and power,
by the great Singer painted,
by the high Powers fashioned,
graved by the Utterer of gods.
BRAY

144. Runes thou wilt find,
and explained characters,
very large characters,
very potent characters,
which the great speaker depicted,
and the high powers formed,
and the powers' prince graved:
THORPE

143. Runes shalt thou find, and fateful signs,
that the king of singers colored,
and the mighty gods have made;
Full strong the signs, full mighty the signs,
that the ruler of gods doth write.
BELLOWS

143. Óðinn með ásum,
en fyr alfum Dáinn,
Dvalinn ok dvergum fyrir,
Ásviðr jötnum fyrir,
ek reist sjalfr sumar.

142. For gods graved Odin,
for elves graved Daïn,
Dvalin the Dallier for dwarfs,
All-wise for Jötuns, and I, of myself,
graved some for the sons of men.
BRAY

145. Odin among the Æsir,
but among the Alfar, Dáin,
and Dvalin for the dwarfs,
Ásvid for the Jötuns:
some I myself graved.
THORPE

144. Odin for the gods,
Dain for the elves,
and Dvalin for the dwarfs,
Alsvith for giants and all mankind,
and some myself I wrote.
BELLOWS

144. Veistu, hvé rísta skal?
Veistu, hvé ráða skal?
Veistu, hvé fáa skal?
Veistu, hvé freista skal?
Veistu, hvé biðja skal?
Veistu, hvé blóta skal?
Veistu, hvé senda skal?
Veistu, hvé sóa skal?

143. Dost know how to write,
dost know how to read,
dost know how to paint,
dost know how to prove,
dost know how to ask,
dost know how to offer,
dost know how to send,
dost know how to spend?
BRAY

146. Knowest thou how to grave them?
knowest thou how to expound them?
knowest thou how to depict them?
knowest thou how to prove them?
knowest thou how to pray?
knowest thou how to offer?
knowest thou how to send?
knowest thou how to consume?
THORPE

145. Knowest how one shall write?
knowest how one shall rede?
Knowest how one shall tint?
Knowest how one makes trial?
Knowest how one shall ask?
knowest how one shall offer?
Knowest how one shall send?
Knowest how one shall sacrifice?
BELLOWS

145. Betra er óbeðit
en sé ofblótit,
ey sér til gildis gjöf;
betra er ósent
en sé ofsóit.
Svá Þundr of reist
fyr þjóða rök,
þar hann upp of reis,
er hann aftr of kom.

144. Better ask for too little,
than offer too much,
like the gift should be the boon;
better not to send than to overspend.
Thus Odin graved ere the world began;
Then he rose from the deep, and came again.
BRAY

147. 'Tis better not to pray
than too much offer;
a gift ever looks to a return.
'Tis better not to send
than too much consume.
So Thund graved
before the origin of men,
where he ascended,
to whence he afterwards came.
THORPE

146. Better no prayer,
than too big an offering,
by thy getting measure thy gift;
Better is none than too big a sacrifice;
So Thund of old wrote ere man's race began,
where he rose on high when home he came.
BELLOWS

146. Ljóð ek þau kann,
er kann-at þjóðans kona
ok mannskis mögr.
Hjalp heitir eitt,
en þat þér hjalpa mun
við sökum ok sorgum
ok sútum görvöllum.

145. Those songs I know,
which nor sons of men
nor queen in a king's court knows;
the first is Help which will bring thee help
in all woes and in sorrow and strife.
BRAY

148. Those songs I know
which the king's wife knows not
nor son of man.
Help the first is called,
for that will help thee
against strifes and cares.
THORPE

147. The songs I know,
that king's wives know not,
nor men that are sons of men;
The first is called help,
and help it can bring thee,
in sorrow and pain and sickness.
BELLOWS

147. Þat kann ek annat,
er þurfu ýta synir,
þeir er vilja læknar lifa.

146. A second I know,
which the son of men
must sing, who would heal the sick.
BRAY

149. For the second I know,
what the sons of men require,
who will as leeches live.
THORPE

148. A second I know,
that men shall need,
who leechcraft long to use.
BELLOWS

148. Það kann ek þriðja:
ef mér verðr þörf mikil
hafts við mína heiftmögu,
eggjar ek deyfi
minna andskota,
bíta-t þeim vápn né velir.

147. A third I know:
if sore need should come
of a spell to stay my foes;
when I sing that song,
which shall blunt their swords,
nor their weapons nor staves can wound.
BRAY

150. For the third I know,
if I have great need
to restrain my foes,
the weapons' edge I deaden;
of my adversaries
nor arms nor wiles harm aught.
THORPE

149. A third I know,
if great is my need of fetters to hold my foe;
Blunt do I make mine enemy's blade,
nor bites his sword or staff.
BELLOWS

149. Þat kann ek it fjórða:
ef mér fyrðar bera
bönd að boglimum,
svá ek gel,
at ek ganga má,
sprettr mér af fótum fjöturr,
en af höndum haft.

148. A fourth I know: if men make fast
in chains the joints of my limbs,
when I sing that song which shall set me free,
spring the fetters from hands and feet.
BRAY

151. For the forth I know,
if men place
bonds on my limbs,
I so sing that I can walk;
the fetter starts from my feet,
and the manacle from my hands.
THORPE

150. A fourth I know,
if men shall fasten bonds on my bended legs;
So great is the charm that forth I may go,
the fetters spring from my feet,
broken the bonds from my hands.
BELLOWS

150. Þat kann ek it fimmta:
ef ek sé af fári skotinn
flein í folki vaða,
fýgr-a hann svá stinnt,
at ek stöðvig-a-k,
ef ek hann sjónum of sék.

149. A fifth I know: when I see, by foes shot,
speeding a shaft through the host,
flies it never so strongly I still can stay it,
if I get but a glimpse of its flight.
BRAY

152. For the fifth I know,
I see a shot from a hostile hand,
a shaft flying amid the host,
so swift it cannot fly
that I cannot arrest it,
if only I get sight of it.
THORPE

151. A fifth I know,
if I see from afar an arrow fly against the folk;
It flies not so swift that I stop it not,
if ever my eyes behold it.
BELLOWS

151. Þat kann ek it sétta:
ef mik særir þegn
á vrótum hrás viðar,
ok þann hal
er mik heifta kveðr,
þann eta mein heldr en mik.

150. A sixth I know:
when some thane would harm me
in runes on a moist tree's root,
on his head alone shall light the ills
of the curse that he called upon mine.
BRAY

153. For the sixth I know,
if one wounds me
with a green tree's roots;
also if a man
declares hatred to me,
harm shall consume them sooner than me.
THORPE

152. A sixth I know,
if harm one seeks,
with a sapling's roots to send me;
The hero himself,
who wreaks his hate shall taste the ill ere I.
BELLOWS

152. Þat kann ek it sjaunda:
ef ek sé hávan loga
sal of sessmögum,
brennr-at svá breitt,
at ek hánum bjargig-a-k;
þann kann ek galdr at gala.

151. A seventh I know: if I see a hall
high o'er the bench-mates blazing,
flame it ne'er so fiercely I still can save it,
I know how to sing that song.
BRAY

154. For the seventh I know,
if a lofty house I see
blaze o'er its inmates,
so furiously it shall not burn
that I cannot save it.
That song I can sing.
THORPE

153. A seventh I know,
if I see in flames the hall,
o'er my comrades' heads;
It burns not so wide that I will not quench it,
I know that song to sing.
BELLOWS

153. Þat kann ek it átta,
er öllum er
nytsamligt at nema:
hvars hatr vex
með hildings sonum
þat má ek bæta brátt.

152. An eighth I know: which all can sing
for their weal if they learn it well;
where hate shall wax 'mid the warrior sons,
I can calm it soon with that song.
BRAY

155. For the eighth I know,
what to all is
useful to learn:
where hatred grows
among the sons of men
that I can quickly assuage.
THORPE

154. An eighth I know,
that is to all of greatest good to learn;
When hatred grows among heroes sons,
I soon can set it right.
BELLOWS

154. Þat kann ek it níunda:
ef mik nauðr of stendr
at bjarga fari mínu á floti,
vind ek kyrri
vági á
ok svæfik allan sæ.

153. A ninth I know:
when need befalls me
to save my vessel afloat,
I hush the wind on the stormy wave,
and soothe all the sea to rest.
BRAY

156. For the ninth I know,
if I stand in need
my bark on the water to save,
I can the wind
on the waves allay,
and the sea lull.
THORPE

155. A ninth I know,
if need there comes,
to shelter my ship on the flood;
The wind I calm upon the waves,
and the sea I put to sleep.
BELLOWS

155. Þat kann ek it tíunda:
ef ek sé túnriður
leika lofti á,
ek svá vinnk,
at þær villar fara
sinna heimhama,
sinna heimhuga.

154. A tenth I know:
when at night the witches
ride and sport in the air,
such spells I weave that they wander home
out of skins and wits bewildered.
BRAY

157. For the tenth I know,
if I see troll-wives
sporting in air,
I can so operate
that they will forsake
their own forms,
and their own minds.
THORPE

156. A tenth I know,
what time I see house-riders flying on high;
So can I work that wildly they go,
showing their true shapes,
hence to their own homes.
BELLOWS

156. Þat kann ek it ellifta:
ef ek skal til orrostu
leiða langvini,
und randir ek gel,
en þeir með ríki fara
heilir hildar til,
heilir hildi frá,
koma þeir heilir hvaðan.

155. An eleventh I know: if haply I lead
my old comrades out to war,
I sing 'neath the shields, and they fare forth mightily
safe into battle,
safe out of battle,
and safe return from the strife.
BRAY

158. For the eleventh I know,
if I have to lead
my ancient friends to battle,
under their shields I sing,
and with power they go
safe to the fight,
safe from the fight;
safe on every side they go.
THORPE

157. An eleventh I know,
if needs I must lead to the fight my long-loved friends;
I sing in the shields, and in strength they go
whole to the field of fight,
whole from the field of fight,
and whole they come thence home.
BELLOWS

157. Þat kann ek it tolfta:
ef ek sé á tré uppi
váfa virgilná,
svá ek ríst
ok í rúnum fák,
at sá gengr gumi
ok mælir við mik.

156. A twelfth I know: if I see in a tree
a corpse from a halter hanging,
such spells I write, and paint in runes,
that the being descends and speaks.
BRAY

159. For the twelfth I know,
if on a tree I see
a corpse swinging from a halter,
I can so grave
and in runes depict,
that the man shall walk,
and with me converse.
THORPE

158. A twelfth I know,
if high on a tree I see a hanged man swing;
So do I write and color the runes,
that forth he fares, and to me talks.
BELLOWS

158. Þat kann ek it þrettánda:
ef ek skal þegn ungan
verpa vatni á,
mun-at hann falla,
þótt hann í folk komi,
hnígr-a sá halr fyr hjörum.

157. A thirteenth I know:
if the new-born son
of a warrior I sprinkle with water,
that youth will not fail when he fares to war,
never slain shall he bow before sword.
BRAY

160. For the thirteenth I know,
if on a young man
I sprinkle water,
he shall not fall,
though he into battle come:
that man shall not sink before swords.
THORPE

159. A thirteenth I know,
if a thane full young,
with water I sprinkle well;
He shall not fall,
though he fares mid the host,
nor sink beneath the swords.
BELLOWS

159. Þat kann ek it fjögurtánda:
ef ek skal fyrða liði
telja tíva fyrir,
ása ok alfa
ek kann allra skil;
fár kann ósnotr svá.

158. A fourteenth I know:
if I needs must number
the Powers to the people of men,
I know all the nature of gods and of elves
which none can know untaught.
BRAY

161. For the fourteenth I know,
if in the society of men
I have to enumerate the gods,
Æsir and Alfar,
I know the distinctions of all.
This few unskilled can do.
THORPE

160. A fourteenth I know,
if fain I would name to men the mighty gods;
All know I well of the gods and elves,
few be the fools know this.
BELLOWS

160. Þat kann ek it fimmtánda
er gól Þjóðrerir
dvergr fyr Dellings durum:
afl gól hann ásum,
en alfum frama,
hyggju Hroftatý.

159. A fifteenth I know,
which Folk-stirrer sang,
the dwarf, at the gates of Dawn;
he sang strength to the gods,
and skill to the elves,
and wisdom to Odin who utters.
BRAY

162. For the fifteenth I know
what the dwarf Thiodreyrir sang
before Delling's doors.
Strength he sang to the Æsir,
and to the Alfar prosperity,
wisdom to Hroptatýr.
THORPE

161. A fifteenth I know,
that before the doors of Delling,
sang Thjothrorir the dwarf;
Might he sang for the gods,
and glory for elves,
and wisdom for Hroptatyr wise.
BELLOWS

161. Þat kann ek it sextánda:
ef ek vil ins svinna mans
hafa geð allt ok gaman,
hugi ek hverfi
hvítarmri konu,
ok sný ek hennar öllum sefa.

160. A sixteenth I know:
when all sweetness and love
I would win from some artful wench,
her heart I turn, and the whole mind change
of that fair-armed lady I love.
BRAY

163. For the sixteenth I know,
if a modest maiden's favour and affection
I desire to possess,
the soul I change
of the white-armed damsel,
and wholly turn her mind.
THORPE

162. A sixteenth I know,
if I seek delight to win from a maiden wise;
The mind I turn of the white-armed maid,
and thus change all her thoughts.
BELLOWS

162. Þat kann ek it sjautjánda
at mik mun seint firrask
it manunga man.
Ljóða þessa
mun þú, Loddfáfnir,
lengi vanr vera;
þó sé þér góð, ef þú getr,
nýt ef þú nemr,
þörf ef þú þiggr.

161. A seventeenth I know:
so that e'en the shy maiden
is slow to shun my love.
BRAY

162. These songs, Stray-Singer,
which man's son knows not,
long shalt thou lack in life,
though thy weal if thou win'st them,
thy boon if thou obey'st them
thy good if haply thou gain'st them.
BRAY

164. For the seventeenth I know,
that that young maiden will
reluctantly avoid me.
These songs, Loddfafnir!
thou wilt long have lacked;
yet it may be good if thou understandest them,
profitable if thou learnest them.
THORPE

163. A seventeenth I know,
so that seldom shall go a maiden young from me
BELLOWS

164. Long these songs thou shalt,
Loddfafnir, seek in vain to sing;
Yet good it be if thou mightest get them,
Well, if thou wouldst them learn,
Help, if thou hadst them.
BELLOWS

163. Þat kann ek it átjánda,
er ek æva kennik
mey né manns konu,
- allt er betra,
er einn of kann;
þat fylgir ljóða lokum, -
nema þeiri einni,
er mik armi verr,
eða mín systir sé.

163. An eighteenth I know:
which I ne'er shall tell
to maiden or wife of man
save alone to my sister, or haply to her
who folds me fast in her arms;
most safe are secrets known to but one-
the songs are sung to an end.
BRAY

165. For the eighteenth I know
that which I never teach
to maid or wife of man,
(all is better
what one only knows.
This is the closing of the songs)
save her alone
who clasps me in her arms,
or is my sister.
THORPE

165. An eighteenth I know,
that ne'er will I tell to maiden or wife of man,
the best is what none but one's self doth know;
So comes the end of the songs,
save only to her in whose arms I lie,
or who else my sister is.
BELLOWS

164. Nú eru Háva mál
kveðin Háva höllu í,
allþörf ýta sonum,
óþörf jötna sonum;
heill sá, er kvað,
heill sá, er kann,
njóti sá, er nam,
heilir, þeirs hlýddu.

164. Now the sayings of the High One,
are uttered in the hall
for the weal of men, f
or the woe of Jötuns,
Hail, thou who hast spoken!
Hail, thou that knowest!
Hail, ye that have hearkened!
Use, thou who hast learned!
BRAY

166. Now are sung the
High-one's songs,
in the High-one's hall,
to the sons of men all-useful,
but useless to the Jötun's sons.
Hail to him who has sung them!
Hail to him who knows them!
May he profit who has learnt them!
Hail to hose who have listened to them!
THORPE

138. Now are Hor's words spoken in the hall,
kind for the kindred of men,
Cursed for the kindred of giants:
Hail to the speaker, and to him who learns!
Profit be his who has them!
Hail to them who hearken!
BELLOWS

Made in the USA
Coppell, TX
05 August 2023